888 Hints for the Home

888 Tipps für Ihr Zuhause

888 Woonideeën

888 Hints for the Home

888 Tipps für Ihr Zuhause

888 Woonideeën

FKG

F K G

Editorial project:
2011 © LOFT Publications
Via Laietana, 32, 4.º, of. 92
08003 Barcelona, Spain
Tel.: +34 932 688 088
Fax: +34 932 687 073
loft@loftpublications.com
www.loftpublications.com

Created and distributed in cooperation with Frechmann Kolón GmbH
www.frechmann.com

Editor:
Daniela Santos Quartino

Editorial coordinator:
Simone K. Schleifer

Assistant to editorial coordination:
Aitana Lleonart Triquell

Art director:
Mireia Casanovas Soley

Design and layout coordination:
Claudia Martínez Alonso

Layout:
Anabel N. Quintana

Cover layout:
María Eugenia Castell Carballo

Translations:
Cillero & de Motta, Mengès (FR)

ISBN 978-84-9936-003-4 (GB)
ISBN 978-84-9936-000-3 (D)
ISBN 978-84-9936-057-7 (NL)

Printed in China

Few things are as stressful and as exciting as moving house. Empty spaces create the same anxiety that an artist suffers in front of a blank canvas. So much to do and so many possibilities!

So, beyond the style that the house will have – which is very important to establish from the outset –, there are a number of guidelines that can help us to optimally distribute the spaces, to efficiently position the fittings and successfully organize the furniture.

All these ideas are reflected in this book, which covers, chapter by chapter, the different living spaces, and includes tips, tricks and advice on decorative details and the colors and textures suitable for any area of the house.

Wenige Dinge sind so anstrengend und gleichzeitig aufregend wie ein Umzug. Leere Räume lösen dieselbe innere Unruhe aus, die ein Künstler vor einer weißen Leinwand empfindet. Es ist so viel zu tun, und es gibt so viele Möglichkeiten!

Deshalb gibt es neben dem Stil, in dem die Wohnung gestaltet werden soll, - und es ist wichtig, darüber von Anfang an zu entscheiden – eine Reihe von Richtlinien, die uns dabei helfen können, die Räume optimal aufzuteilen, die Einrichtung effektiv zu gestalten und die Möbel so aufzustellen, dass wir uns wohlfühlen.

Alle diese Ideen sind in diesem Buch vereint, das Kapitel für Kapitel die verschiedenen Räume der Wohnung durchgeht, und sie werden mit Ideen, Tricks und Ratschlägen zu dekorativen Details, geeigneten Farben und Texturen für jede Fläche des Hauses ergänzt.

Peu d'expériences sont aussi stressantes et excitantes à la fois que celle qui consiste à changer de maison. Les espaces vides provoquent la même anxiété que celle qu'éprouve un artiste devant la toile blanche. Tout est à faire et il y a tellement de possibilités !

C'est la raison pour laquelle, au-delà du style qu'il est important de choisir dès le début, il existe une série de modèles pouvant nous aider à optimiser la distribution des espaces, à placer les équipements aux meilleurs endroits et à organiser l'emplacement du mobilier.

Cet ouvrage parcourt, chapitre par chapitre, les différentes pièces, offrant suggestions, astuces et conseils sur la décoration, les couleurs et les matériaux adaptés.

Weinig dingen zijn zo stressvol en opwindend tegelijkertijd als verhuizen. Lege ruimtes roepen dezelfde angst op als die een schilder voelt voor een wit doek. Alles moet nog gemaakt worden en er zijn zo veel mogelijkheden!

Daarom zijn er, naast de stijl die de woning zal hebben – en waarover al in het beginstadium moet worden beslist – een aantal richtsnoeren die ons kunnen helpen om de ruimtes optimaal in te delen, de voorzieningen op efficiënte wijze te plaatsen en de woning naar tevredenheid in te richten.

Al deze ideeën zijn opgenomen in dit boek, dat per hoofdstuk de verschillende vertrekken van de woning bij langs gaat en ideeën, trucs en tips geeft over decoratieve details en de geschikte kleuren en texturen voor iedere willekeurige ruimte van de woning.

LIVING ROOM
WOHNZIMMER
SALON
ZITKAMER

To define the living room in spaces shared with other areas of the house, organize the space around these three basic elements: a sofa, coffee table and rug.

Um das Wohnzimmer von anderen Bereichen innerhalb der Wohnung abzugrenzen, sollte man die Proportionen zwischen diesen drei Grundelementen beachten: Das Sofa, den Couchtisch und den Teppich.

Pour délimiter le salon dans un espace partagé avec d'autres zones de la maison, il faut maintenir les proportions entre les formes de ces trois éléments de base : le canapé, la table basse et le tapis.

Om de zitkamer binnen ruimtes die gedeeld worden met andere entourages van de woning af te bakenen, moeten de juiste proporties van de vormen van deze basiselementen te worden aangehouden: de bank, de zitkamertafel en het vloerkleed.

A chaise longue is perfect to separate spaces. As it does not have a back there will be a better flow of communication between the different zones.

Stellen Sie eine *chaise longe* auf, um die Bereiche zu voneinander zu trennen. Da sie keine Rücklehne hat, ermöglicht sie eine bessere Kommunikation zwischen den verschiedenen Wohnbereichen.

Pour séparer les différentes zones, on utilise une chaise longue qui, n'ayant pas de dossier, permet une meilleure communication entre les espaces.

Gebruik een *chaise longe* om vertrekken van elkaar te scheiden. Zonder rugleuning lijken de verschillende ruimtes meer met elkaar verbonden.

Fit a mirror behind the couch that fills the entire wall to dramatically create the feeling of spaciousness in the living room. This tip is only suitable for minimalist ambiences, as otherwise the space would be too overelaborate.

Bringen Sie hinter dem Sessel einen Spiegel an, der die gesamte Wand einnimmt. Dadurch wirkt das Wohnzimmer sehr viel größer. Dieser Trick ist nur für Zimmer geeignet, die minimalistisch eingerichtet sind, im anderen Fall wirkt der Raum überfüllt.

Placer un grand miroir sur tout le mur derrière le canapé permet d'augmenter de façon spectaculaire la sensation d'espace dans le salon. Cette astuce n'est valable que dans les pièces minimalistes, sinon elle pourrait provoquer un effet final trop chargé.

Plaats een spiegel die de hele wand achter de fauteuil inneemt, zodat het lijkt alsof de zitkamer veel groter is. Deze truc is alleen geschikt voor minimalistische vertrekken omdat de ruimte anders te vol lijkt.

Make openings in the wall above the windows when the ceilings of the house are very high. In addition to light, these additional windows provide heat in winter and extra ventilation in summer.

Wenn die Decken der Wohnung sehr hoch sind, bauen Sie Öffnungen oberhalb der Fenster ein. Diese zusätzlichen Fenster lassen nicht nur mehr Licht ein, sondern sorgen im Winter für mehr Wärme und im Sommer für Lüftung.

Un plafond très haut permet d'insérer des ouvertures dans le mur au-dessus des fenêtres : elles augmentent la luminosité de la pièce, apportent de la chaleur en hiver et permettent à l'air de mieux circuler en été.

Maak openingen in de muur boven de ramen als het huis heel hoge plafonds heeft. Behalve licht geven deze extra ramen ook warmte in de winter en extra ventilatie in de zomer.

Instead of a central light fixture in the ceiling, create points of light in different parts of the living room with lamps that hang from key corners to create several ambiences.

Anstatt einer zentralen Deckenlampe installieren Sie Lichtquellen an verschiedenen Stellen des Wohnzimmers mit Hängelampen über Kernbereichen, um unterschiedliche Stimmungen zu schaffen.

Au lieu de fixer un lustre au centre du plafond, on peut créer des points de lumière dans différentes parties du salon avec des lampes installées à des endroits clé, qui vont générer des ambiances variées.

Installeer, in plaats van een centrale plafondlamp, lichtpunten op verschillende plaatsen in de zitkamer door lampen boven belangrijke plekken te hangen. Zo ontstaan er verschillende sferen.

Take advantage of irregularities in the house to install certain furniture or equipment, such as the stove and space to store wood.

Nutzen Sie Niveauunterschiede in der Wohnung aus, um bestimmte Möbel oder Gegenstände wie den Ofen und Feuerholz unterzubringen.

Les dénivelés de la maison peuvent accueillir certains meubles ou équipements comme le poêle et servir d'espace de rangement pour le bois.

Maak van de niveauverschillen in het huis gebruik om bepaalde meubels of gebruiksvoorwerpen, zoals de kachel, neer te zetten of om brandhout op te slaan.

Use original coffee tables such as a footrest or old recycled suitcases to give character to this area of the house.

Verwenden Sie originelle Stücke als Couchtisch wie Fußstützen oder alte aufgearbeitete Koffer, um dem Zimmer eine persönliche Note zu verleihen.

Des tables basses originales, comme un repose-pieds ou des vieilles malles, donnent du caractère à cette partie de la maison.

Neem uw toevlucht tot originele salontafels zoals voetsteunen of oude gerecyclede koffers, om dit vertrek van de woning een persoonlijk tintje te geven.

Occupy an entire wall of the living room with a bookcase.
Why leave an empty space around a small shelf?

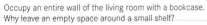

Stellen Sie ein Bücherregal auf, das eine gesamte Wand
des Wohnzimmers einnimmt. Warum sollte man um ein
kleines Regal herum weiße Stellen frei lassen?

On utilise le mur du salon pour installer une bibliothèque
qui occupe toute la surface. Pourquoi laisser de l'espace
vide autour d'un petit meuble ?

Gebruik een hele wand van de zitkamer als boekenkast
die het hele muuroppervlak in beslag neemt. Waarom
zou u ruimte open laten rond een kleine boekenkast?

The side walls of a wood-burning stove are ideal for installing shelves for books, pictures and ornaments.

Die Seitenwände eines Holzofens sind ideal für den Einbau von Fächern, um darin Bücher, Fotos und Ziergegenstände aufzustellen.

Les parois latérales d'un poêle à bois sont l'endroit idéal pour installer des étagères et créer une bibliothèque où ranger des livres, des photos et des objets de décoration.

De muren naast de houtkachel zijn ideaal om planken te bevestigen en een wandmeubel voor boeken, foto's en decoratieve elementen neer te zetten.

Match the color and material of the bookcase and the coffee table to create a strong ensemble from a stylistic point of view.

Kombinieren Sie Farbe und Material des Bücherregals und des Couchtischs, um ein stilistisch überzeugendes Ensemble zu schaffen.

La couleur et le matériau de la bibliothèque s'harmonisent avec la table basse créant un ensemble au style assuré.

Combineer de kleur en het materiaal van de boekenkast en de salontafel om een uit stilistisch oogpunt overtuigend geheel te creëren.

Take advantage of an opening in the walls of the living room to fit shelves (glass if possible to allow light to pass freely between the rooms).

Nutzen Sie eine Öffnung in der Wohnzimmerwand, um Regale aufzustellen. Diese sollten aus Glas sein, damit sie Licht in die Räume lassen.

Une ouverture dans les murs du salon peut accueillir des étagères en verre permettant à la lumière de circuler librement.

Benut openingen in de wanden van de zitkamer om planken te bevestigen. Maak deze van glas voor meer lichtinval tussen de verschillende ruimtes

Make the bottom shelf of the bookcase wider so that it can be used as an office desk.

Bringen Sie unterhalb des Bücherregals ein breiteres Regalbrett an, das Sie als Schreibtisch benutzen können.

On peut monter une étagère plus large dans la partie basse de la bibliothèque pour la transformer en table de travail.

Plaats een bredere plank onderaan de boekenkast, die dienst kan doen als tafel voor de werkruimte.

Install a shelf about 15.8 inches off the floor in a corner of the living room that you can use as a table or bench.

Installieren Sie in einer Ecke des Wohnzimmers in ca. 40 cm Höhe ein Regalbrett. Sie gewinnen damit eine Fläche, die Sie als Beistelltisch oder Bank nutzen können.

Installer une étagère dans un coin du salon à environ 40 cm du sol permet de gagner une surface utilisable comme petite table ou banquette.

Installeer een plank op ongeveer 40 cm van de vloer in een hoek van de zitkamer. Zo krijgt u een extra oppervlak dat gebruikt kan worden als tafeltje of bank.

Create more storage space on the wall behind the sofa. Choose a shelf length equal in length or longer than the sofa and install it high enough so that it does not get in the way.

Nutzen Sie die Wand, an der sich das Sofa befindet, um Stellplatz zu gewinnen. Suchen Sie ein Regalbrett aus, das genauso lang oder länger als das Sofa ist, und bringen Sie es hoch genug an, dass man sich nicht daran stoßen kann.

Le mur occupé par le canapé permet d'optimiser l'espace de rangement. On choisit une étagère d'une largeur égale ou supérieure à celle du canapé et on la monte à une hauteur suffisante pour éviter de s'y cogner.

Gebruik de muur waar de bank tegenaan staat als extra opbergruimte. Kies een plank die net zo lang of nog langer is dan de bank en plaats hem hoog genoeg zodat niemand zijn of haar hoofd stoot.

Fit open shelves for ornaments and hide objects and toys that would make the space look messy behind doors.

Lassen Sie einige Fächer der Schrankwand für Ziergegenstände offen, und bewahren Sie hinter den Türen Papiere, Spielzeug und Gegenstände auf, die dem Zimmer sonst ein unordentliches Aussehen geben würden.

Vous pouvez disposer les objets de décoration sur des étagères ouvertes et ranger à l'intérieur les papiers, les jouets et d'autres éléments qui donneraient un aspect désordonné à l'espace.

Zet accessoires op de planken en bewaar papieren, voorwerpen en speelgoed die het vertrek een slordig uiterlijk geven achter de deuren van het meubelstuk.

Rustic flooring such as terracotta or polished concrete creates warmth in contrast to textiles and rugs from natural fibers.

Rustikale Böden aus Terrakotta oder aus poliertem Zement wirken im Kontrast mit Textilien und Teppichen aus Naturfasern wärmer.

Les revêtements de sol rustiques comme la terre cuite ou le béton poli sont mis en valeur par les tissus et les tapis en fibres naturelles.

Vloeren met landelijke plavuizen zoals terracotta of gepolijst cement doen warmer aan in contrast met textiel en vloerkleden van natuurlijke vezels.

A rug in the living room in an area where a lot of people pass by should be sturdy and heavy so that it does not move and remains in place.

Ein Wohnzimmerteppich, der viel begangen wird, muss robust und schwer sein, damit er nicht rutscht und fest an seinem Platz liegen bleibt.

Un tapis de salon très exposé au passage doit être solide et lourd pour qu'il reste en place, évitant ainsi qu'il ne glisse.

Een vloerkleed op een loopruimte binnen de zitkamer moet robuust en zwaar zijn, zodat hij niet verschuift en op zijn plaats blijft liggen.

Built-in sofas are ideal for casual or rustic spaces.
A masonry bench must be built and finished off
with cushions of different sizes and shapes.

Eingebaute Sofas sind für rustikale, heitere Räume
geeignet. Dafür wird eine Bank gemauert, auf die
man Kissen verschiedener Größe und Form legt.

Les canapés en maçonnerie sont adaptés aux ambiances
décontractées ou rustiques : il suffit de bâtir une
banquette en maçonnerie et de la compléter avec
des coussins aux formes et aux dimensions variées.

Ingebouwde banken zijn ideaal voor vertrekken met een
nonchalante of landelijke sfeer. Daarvoor moet een bank
worden gemetseld, die later wordt opgesierd met kussen
van verschillende afmetingen en vormen.

Opt for modular sofas by adding or removing pieces such as the chaise longue or the footrest, according to space and use requirements.

Entscheiden Sie sich für mehrteilige Sofas, bei denen man Elemente hinzufügen oder wegnehmen kann, wie die *chaise longe* oder Fußstützen, je nach Platz und Verwendungszweck.

Vous pouvez opter pour des canapés modulables qui permettent d'ajouter ou d'enlever des éléments comme la chaise longue ou le repose-pieds, en accord avec l'espace et vos besoins.

Kies modulaire sofa's waaraan onderdelen, zoals *chaise longe* of voetenbanken kunnen worden toegevoegd of weggehaald, al naar gelang de ruimte en de gebruiksbehoeften.

Sofas with integrated shelves are perfect to have useful objects such as throws, remote controls and books near at hand.

Sofas mit eingebauten Fächern sind sehr praktisch, um häufig gebrauchte Gegenstände, wie Decken, Fernbedienungen und Bücher zur Hand zu haben.

Les canapés avec tablettes intégrées sont très utiles pour garder sous la main les objets les plus utilisés au salon comme les couvertures, les télécommandes et les livres.

Banken met geïntegreerde planken zijn een grote bondgenoot om de meest gebruikte voorwerpen in de zitkamer, zoals dekens, afstandsbediening of boeken, bij de hand te hebben.

Create a living room that is both modern and elegant: let the sofa or the armchairs add color to the room and keep the rest of the space within the same range of contrasting tones.

Gestalten Sie ein elegantes und zugleich modernes Wohnzimmer: Verleihen Sie ihm durch das Sofa und die Sessel eine farbige Note, und halten Sie den übrigen Raum in einem einheitlichen, kontrastierenden Ton.

Comment créer un salon élégant et moderne : la touche de couleur apportée par le canapé ou les fauteuils contraste avec les autres éléments de la pièce qui appartiennent à une même gamme de couleurs.

Creëer een elegante en tegelijkertijd moderne zitkamer: laat de bank of de stoelen voor een kleurig accent zorgen en houd de rest van de ruimte binnen hetzelfde contrasterende kleurengamma.

To enhance a living room in which one tone is dominant, choose a sofa with a contrasting color.

Um den einheitlichen Ton des Wohnzimmers hervorzuheben, wählen Sie für das Sofa eine kontrastierende Farbe.

Pour rehausser la couleur d'un salon où domine une seule tonalité, on choisit un canapé ayant une couleur qui contraste avec celle-ci.

Kies voor een bank in een contrasterende kleur om een zitkamer waarin een kleur overheerst beter te doen uitkomen.

Go for prints on the sofa but keep to the same range
of colors for the rest of the furniture and fittings

Haben Sie Mut zu einem Sofa mit gemustertem
Bezug, aber halten Sie die anderen Möbel und
Einrichtungsgegenstände im gleichen Farbton.

Vous pouvez oser les imprimés pour votre canapé mais
vous devez respecter la même gamme de couleurs pour
les meubles et les équipements restants.

Durf met bedrukte stoffering in de bank, maar houd
daarbij hetzelfde kleurengamma aan als de rest van
de meubels en gebruiksvoorwerpen.

Use fabrics as a decorative element. Simply changing
the combination of cushions, throws and rugs is enough
to give a living room a makeover.

Nutzen Sie Textilien als dekorative Elemente. Es genügt
einfach die Kissen, Decken und Teppiche auszuwechseln,
um dem Wohnzimmer ein neues Aussehen zu verleihen.

Les tissus deviennent des éléments de décoration. Le
salon peut changer d'aspect facilement en coordonnant
différemment les coussins, les couvertures et les tapis.

Neem uw toevlucht tot stoffering als decoratief element.
Door simpelweg de combinatie van kussens, dekens en
vloerkleden te veranderen, geeft u de zitkamer een nieuw
uiterlijk.

Opt for a long, narrow coffee table when you do not have much space in front of the sofa.

Wenn es nicht viel Platz vor dem Sofa gibt, wählen Sie einen länglichen, schmalen Couchtisch.

Lorsque l'espace devant le canapé est réduit, une table basse allongée et étroite est la solution idéale.

Kies een lange en smalle salontafel als de ruimte voor de bank beperkt is.

Combine the coffee table with a smaller, side table
so you can use them for different purposes.

Kombinieren Sie den Couchtisch mit einem kleineren
Beistelltisch, so können Sie sie für verschiedene Zwecke
verwenden.

On peut combiner la table basse centrale avec une
autre plus petite d'appoint et les destiner à des usages
différents.

Combineer de salontafel met een kleinere bijzettafel.
Zo kunnen ze voor verschillende dingen gebruikt worden.

The height of the coffee tables should be the same
height as the armchairs or the sofa.

Die Höhe der Couchtische muss zu der Höhe
der Sessel und des Sofas passen.

La hauteur des tables basses doit être adaptée
à la hauteur des fauteuils ou du canapé.

De hoogte van de salontafel moet passen
bij de hoogte van de stoelen of de bank.

A side table is both functional and decorative. Therefore, when choosing it we can unleash our creativity and recycle pieces that acquire a new use.

Der Beistelltisch ist sowohl nützlich als auch dekorativ. Deshalb können wir bei dessen Auswahl unserer Kreativität freien Lauf lassen und Gegenstände recyceln, die nun eine neue Verwendung finden.

La table d'appoint a aussi bien une fonction pratique que décorative. Par conséquent, vous pouvez donner libre cours à votre créativité en recyclant des éléments auxquels vous attribuez un nouvel usage.

Een bijzettafel is zowel functioneel als decoratief. Laat daarom bij de keuze uw creativiteit de vrije loop en recycle onderdelen die op een andere manier kunnen worden aangewend.

Transparent side tables have the major advantage of not affecting the style of the room. The most important thing is not to place them in areas where they will get in the way.

Durchsichtige Beistelltische haben den großen Vorteil, dass sie den Stil des Wohnzimmers nicht beeinträchtigen. Das Wichtigste ist, sie nicht so aufzustellen, dass sie den Durchgang nicht behindern.

Les tables d'appoint transparentes ont le grand avantage de ne pas interférer avec le style du salon. Le plus important est de ne pas les placer dans les zones de passage pour qu'elles ne gênent pas la circulation.

Doorzichtige bijzettafels hebben als grote voordeel dat ze de stijl van de zitkamer niet beïnvloeden. Het belangrijkste is om ze niet in loopruimtes te plaatsen, zodat ze de doorgang niet belemmeren.

Make the most of the living room area by converting it into a multifunctional space. Place shelves that do not exceed the height of the backrest behind the sofa.

Nutzen Sie die Fläche des Wohnzimmers und verwandeln Sie es in einen Vielzweckraum. Bringen Sie Regale hinter dem Sofa an, die nicht höher als die Rücklehne sind.

On peut rentabiliser les mètres carrés du salon en le transformant en un espace multifonctionnel, avec des étagères derrière le canapé qui ne dépassent pas la hauteur du dossier.

Benut de vierkante meters van de zitkamer door ze in een multifunctionele ruimte om te vormen. Zet boekenkasten achter de bank die niet hoger zijn dan de rugleuning.

A coffee table with wheels can be easily moved and placed where it is required or where it does not get in the way.

Ein Couchtisch mit Rädern kann leicht dahin verschoben werden, wo man ihn am meisten braucht oder wo er am wenigsten stört.

Une table basse à roulettes peut être déplacée facilement et mise à l'endroit le plus utile ou, dans ce cas, le moins gênant.

Een salontafel op wieltjes is gemakkelijk te verplaatsen, zodat u hem daar kunt neerzetten waar u hem nodig heeft, of juist waar hij het minst in de weg staat.

In ambiences with neutral tones, hang different colored curtains on one window to create an interesting play of light in the room.

In Räumen mit neutralen Farbtönen hängen Sie an einem Fenster verschiedenfarbige Vorhänge auf, um ein interessantes Lichtspiel im Zimmer zu schaffen.

Dans un intérieur aux tons neutres, vous pouvez choisir pour une même fenêtre des rideaux de couleurs différentes, créant ainsi un jeu de lumière intéressant dans la pièce.

Hang in ruimtes met neutrale kleurschakeringen voor hetzelfde raam gordijnen in verschillende kleuren op, voor een interessant lichtspel naar binnen toe.

Create a balanced environment. Draw an imaginary horizontal line along the walls and do not used colored elements above the top half of the line.

Schaffen Sie eine ausgeglichene Atmosphäre. Ziehen Sie eine imaginäre horizontale Linie an den Wänden entlang und bringen Sie keine farbigen Elemente oberhalb dieser Linie an.

Vous pouvez créer un ensemble équilibré, en évitant de placer des éléments de couleurs au-dessus d'une ligne imaginaire horizontale tracée sur les murs du salon.

Zorg voor een evenwichtige sfeer. Trek een denkbeeldige horizontale lijn langs de muren en laat kleurelementen niet meer dan de helft van de lijn innemen.

Use curtains to separate spaces or as screens. They can be hung from a thin metal rod attached to the ceiling or on rails.

Benutzen Sie die Vorhänge auch als Trennwände oder Wandschirme. Man kann sie von einer schmalen Metallleiste oder Schienen, die an der Decke befestigt werden, hängen lassen.

On peut utiliser les rideaux comme élément de séparation de l'espace ou comme paravent, les accrochant à une fine barre métallique fixée au plafond ou à des tringles.

Maak ook gebruik van gordijnen of kamerschermen om ruimtes van elkaar te scheiden. Deze kunnen met een dunne metalen stang of rail aan het plafond worden bevestigd.

Roller blinds and shutters are ideal for windows
on walls which are occupied with furniture.

Stores oder Rollos sind ideal für Fenster, die sich
an Wänden befinden, an denen Möbelstücke stehen.

Les stores sont les rideaux parfaits pour des fenêtres
situées dans des murs avec des meubles.

Rolgordijnen en zonneblinden zijn ideale gordijnen
voor ramen in muren waar meubels tegenaan staan.

Instead of placing a floor lamp on the side table in the corner, choose a low-hanging light fixture. In this way, the light covers a wider area.

Statt einer Lampe auf dem Beistelltisch in der Ecke wählen Sie eine Deckenlampe und hängen Sie sie sehr tief. Auf diese Weise hat das Licht einen größeren Radius.

Au lieu de placer une lampe sur pied sur la petite table d'appoint à l'angle de la pièce, vous pouvez accrocher une lampe au plafond et la faire descendre très bas : la lumière rayonnera ainsi sur une surface plus vaste.

Kies, in plaats van een staande lamp op het bijzettafeltje in de hoek voor een plafondlamp en laat deze heel laag hangen. Op die manier wordt het licht beter verspreid.

Place a floor lamp beside the sofa: it is great for reading and also creates an intimate, warm atmosphere.

Stellen Sie eine Stehlampe neben dem Sofa auf: Sie ist sehr praktisch zum lesen und erzeugt außerdem eine intime, gemütliche Atmosphäre.

Mettre un lampadaire à côté du canapé facilite la lecture et crée une atmosphère intime et accueillante.

Zet een staande lamp naast de bank: heel geschikt om bij te lezen en eveneens voor een intieme en gezellige sfeer.

Place a desk behind the backrest of the sofa to save space.

Bringen Sie den Schreibtisch an der Rücklehne des Sofas an, um Platz zu sparen.

Appuyer la table de travail contre le dossier du canapé permet de gagner de la place.

Zet de werktafel tegen de achterkant van de bank om ruimte te besparen.

Use the space under the staircase to create a work area. Opt for a narrow desk or make it using a shelf supported on trestles.

Nutzen die den Platz unter der Treppe um einen Arbeitsplatz zu schaffen. Wählen Sie schmale Tische, oder errichten Sie sie mit einem Fach auf Böcken.

Vous pouvez utiliser l'espace vide sous les escaliers pour créer une zone de travail : une table étroite ou tout simplement une étagère posée sur les tréteaux fera l'affaire.

Gebruik de ruimte onder de trap als werkruimte. Kies voor smalle tafels of maak er zelf een met een plank op schragen.

Respect the style of the living room when building the
chimney. Current trends are influenced by simple, straight
lines in one color.

Wenn Sie den Kamin bauen, berücksichtigen Sie den Stil
des Wohnzimmers. In den aktuellen Tendenzen herrschen
die einfachen, geraden, Formen und Einfarbigkeit vor.

La cheminée doit respecter le style du salon. Les
tendances actuelles présentent des formes simples,
droites et d'une couleur unie.

Respecteer de stijl van de zitkamer als u een open haard
wilt aanleggen. De huidige trends schrijven eenvoudige en
rechte vormen met een kleur voor.

If you install a chimney in a corner you will save space in the living room.

Wenn Sie den Kamin in einer Ecke installieren, gewinnen Sie Platz im Wohnzimmer.

Installer la cheminée dans un coin du salon permet d'optimiser l'espace.

Door de open haard in een hoek te installeren creëert u meer ruimte in de zitkamer.

Use the chimney to build a panel that partially divides the spaces.

Nutzen Sie den Kamin um ein Paneel zu bauen, das die Räume unterteilt.

On peut utiliser la cheminée pour construire une cloison séparant partiellement l'espace.

Gebruik de open haard als paneel om de ruimtes gedeeltelijk van elkaar te scheiden.

As an extension of the chimney, fit a built-in bench scattered with cushions. This will be one of the coziest areas in the house.

Mauern Sie eine Bank als Verlängerung des Kamins, legen Sie ein paar Kissen darauf, und das Ergebnis ist einer der gemütlichsten Räume des Hauses.

Construire une banquette en maçonnerie prolongeant la cheminée et la recouvrir de coussins permet d'obtenir l'un des lieux les plus accueillants de la maison.

Maak een gemetselde bank in het verlengde van de haard, leg er een paar kussens op; dit geeft een gezellig hoekje in het huis.

Hanging pictures is not the only option. Rest them against furniture, shelves or the floor and change their position whenever you want.

Die Bilder aufzuhängen, ist nicht die einzige Option. Lehnen Sie sie gegen Möbelstücke, Regale oder stellen Sie sie auf den Boden, so können Sie sie einfach umstellen, wann immer Sie wollen.

Accrocher les tableaux n'est pas la seule option. Vous pouvez les poser sur les meubles, les étagères ou le sol et les changer de place quand vous le souhaitez.

Schilderijen ophangen is niet de enige mogelijkheid. Laat ze tegen meubels of planken leunen of zet ze op de grond en verzet ze zo vaak u wilt.

Use colors to define the living room in relation to other connected spaces.

Benutzen Sie Farben, um das Wohnzimmer gegenüber den anderen Räumen, mit dem es verbunden ist, abzugrenzen.

Les couleurs peuvent aider à délimiter le salon par rapport aux autres espaces auxquels il est relié.

Neem uw toevlucht tot kleuren om de zitkamer de definiëren met betrekking tot de andere ruimtes waarmee hij verbonden is.

Use large cushions to create informal seating around the table in the living room.

Verwenden Sie feste, dicke Kissen, um unkonventionelle Sitzgelegenheiten um den Couchtisch des Wohnzimmers herum zu gestalten.

Des coussins fermes et très volumineux deviennent des sièges informels autour de la table basse centrale du salon.

Kies voor stevige kussens van groot formaat om informele zitplaatsen rond de salontafel van de zithoek in te richten.

On the walls where the heating panels are situated, place two armchairs instead of a sofa, so that the heat radiates easier in the room.

Stellen Sie Sessel statt einem Sofa an die Wände, an denen sich die Heizkörper befinden, damit die Wärme sich leichter im Raum verbreiten kann.

Placer des fauteuils au lieu d'un canapé contre le mur où se trouvent les radiateurs permet à la chaleur de se diffuser plus facilement.

Zet twee stoelen in plaats van een bank tegen de muren waar de verwarming is geïnstalleerd, zodat de warmte beter door de ruimte kan stromen.

Move the sofa away from the wall in a diagonal position. Make use of the space created against the wall to place a designer lamp.

Rücken Sie das Sofa von der Wand ab, und stellen Sie es diagonal. An den so an der Wand geschaffenen Platz stellen Sie eine Designerlampe auf.

Vous pouvez éloigner le canapé du mur et le placer en diagonal pour utiliser l'espace créé avec la paroi et poser une lampe design.

Zet de bank schuin en iets van de muur af. Benut de verkregen ruimte bij de muur om een designlamp neer te zetten.

The size of living room can be increased substantially if it is properly connected with the front porch through sliding doors.

Das Wohnzimmer kann erheblich vergrößert werden, wenn man es durch Schiebetüren mit der Veranda verbindet.

Des portes coulissantes reliant directement le porche au salon permettent d'augmenter sensiblement la taille de l'espace à l'intérieur.

De zitkamer lijkt aanzienlijk groter als hij op geschikte wijze doorloopt in de veranda van het huis via schuifdeuren.

HALLS AND PASSAGEWAYS

EINGANGS- UND
DURCHGANGSBEREICHE

ENTRÉES, ESCALIERS ET ZONES
DE PASSAGE

INGANG EN LOOPRUIMTES

Install a decorative element to define the hall. Large or original ceiling lamps occupy very little space.

Stellen Sie ein dekoratives Element auf, um den Eingangsbereich zu definieren. Die Deckenlampen in unterschiedlichen Größen und originellen Formen haben den Vorteil, dass sie sehr wenig Platz einnehmen.

Un élément de décoration permet de délimiter l'entrée. Les lampes de plafond aux dimensions ou aux formes originales présentent l'avantage d'occuper très peu de place.

Zet een decoratief element neer om de entree te definiëren. Hanglampen van grote afmetingen of met originele vormen hebben als voordeel dat ze weinig ruimte innemen.

In a low-ceilinged entrance, opt for light-colored cladding and furniture to create the illusion of more space.

In einem Eingangsbereich mit niedrigen Decken sollte man für Wände und Möbel helle Farben wählen, damit der Raum größer wirkt.

Dans une entrée au plafond bas, il vaut mieux choisir un revêtement et des meubles clairs pour augmenter la sensation d'espace.

In een entree met een laag plafond is het raadzaam om voor bekledingen en meubilair in lichte kleuren te kiezen, zodat de ruimte groter lijkt.

Make use of elements of the environs to decorate halls and combine them with traditional objects such as mirrors and candelabras.

Nutzen Sie die Elemente der Umgebung um den Eingangsbereich zu dekorieren und kombinieren Sie sie mit traditionellen Gegenständen wie Spiegel und Kerzenleuchtern.

On peut utiliser les éléments de l'environnement pour décorer l'entrée, les associant à des objets traditionnels tels les glaces et les bougeoirs.

Maak gebruik van de elementen in de omgeving om de hal in te richten en combineer deze met traditionele voorwerpen zoals spiegels en kandelaars.

Fringed curtains are a solution to visually separate
environments in a simple way without losing light.
They are also very decorative.

Die Fransengardine ist eine gute Lösung, um die Bereiche
ohne Lichtverlust optische voneinander zu trennen.
Außerdem sind sie sehr dekorativ.

Les rideaux frangés constituent une solution simple
pour séparer visuellement les espaces sans renoncer
à la lumière. De plus, ils sont très décoratifs.

Gordijnen met gerafelde randen vormen een oplossing
om de ruimtes visueel van elkaar te scheiden, zonder dat
ze licht wegnemen. Ze zijn bovendien erg decoratief.

Show your humorous side by fitting a green carpet with
long hair that looks like the lawn in the hall.

Verleihen Sie dem Eingangsbereich Ihres Hauses eine
witzige Note mit einem grünen, langflorigen Teppich,
der wie ein Stück Rasen aussieht.

Vous pouvez ajouter une touche d'humour subtile en
plaçant à l'entrée de la maison un tapis vert à poils longs
imitant le gazon.

Breng een subtiel humoristisch accent aan met een groen,
langharig vloerkleed, waarmee in de entree van
de woning een gazon wordt nagebootst.

Place a small bright-colored chair in the hall, but avoid turning it into a makeshift coat rack on which the coats are thrown upon entering the house.

Stellen Sie einen kleinen Sessel in einer attraktiven Farbe in den Eingangsbereich, aber vermeiden Sie, dass er als improvisierter Kleiderständer benutzt wird, auf den alle Mäntel geworfen werden, sobald man das Haus betritt.

Ce petit fauteuil d'une couleur vive égaye l'entrée. Il faut toutefois éviter qu'il ne se transforme en un portemanteau improvisé où l'on accroche les vêtements dès qu'on accède à la maison.

Zet een kleine fauteuil in een aantrekkelijke kleur bij de ingang, maar zorg ervoor dat deze niet verandert in geïmproviseerde kapstok waar men bij binnenkomst meteen de jas op gooit.

A pair of shelves, a table, a mirror and striking wallpaper are enough to create an original and, above all, a very practical entrance hall.

Ein paar Regalbretter, ein Tischchen, ein Spiegel und eine auffallende Tapete sind ausreichend für einen originellen und vor allem sehr praktischen Empfangsbereich.

Quelques étagères, une petite table, un miroir et du papier peint haut en couleur suffisent à créer une entrée originale et surtout très pratique.

Een paar planken, een tafeltje, een spiegel en een opvallende muur zijn voldoende om en originele en vooral zeer praktische hal te verkrijgen.

Install a built-in book shelf on the wall bordering the front door to place ornaments, boxes to hold keys, letter trays, lamps, etc.

Bauen Sie ein paar Regale in die Wand neben der Eingangstür für Ziergegenstände, Schlüsselkästchen, Fächer für die Post, Lampen, usw., ein.

Sur des étagères en maçonnerie bâties sur la paroi jouxtant la porte d'entrée, on peut placer des objets de décoration, des petites boites à clés, des bacs à courrier, des lampes, etc.

Enkele gemetselde planken aan de muur die grenst aan de voordeur zijn een manier om versieringen, doosjes voor sleutels, bakjes voor de correspondentie, lampen, etc. neer te zetten.

Cantilevered staircases are visually very lightweight and therefore ideal for small environments. The colored steps that contrast with the wall become decorative elements.

Auskragende Treppen wirken sehr leicht und sind daher für kleine Räume geeignet. Stufen, deren Farbe mit der Wand kontrastiert, werden zu dekorativen Elementen.

Visuellement très légers, les escaliers à encorbellement sont adaptés à des espaces réduits. Les marches d'une couleur qui contrastent avec les murs se transforment en éléments de décoration.

Zwevende trappen zien er heel licht uit en zijn daarom ideaal voor kleine ruimtes. De kleurige traptreden contrasteren met de muur en veranderen daardoor in decoratieve elementen.

Give the staircase a special touch with a striking piece of furniture on the landing, whether it is a chair, a small but high table or a lamp.

Geben Sie der Treppe mit einem auffallenden Möbelstück auf dem Absatz, entweder ein Sessel, ein kleiner aber hoher Tisch oder eine Lampe eine besondere Note.

Vous pouvez donner à votre escalier une touche spéciale, en décorant le palier avec un meuble design attrayant – un fauteuil, une petite table haute ou une lampe.

Geef de trap een speciaal accent met een meubelstuk met opvallend ontwerp op de overloop, of kies voor een leunstoel, een klein, maar hoog tafeltje of een lamp.

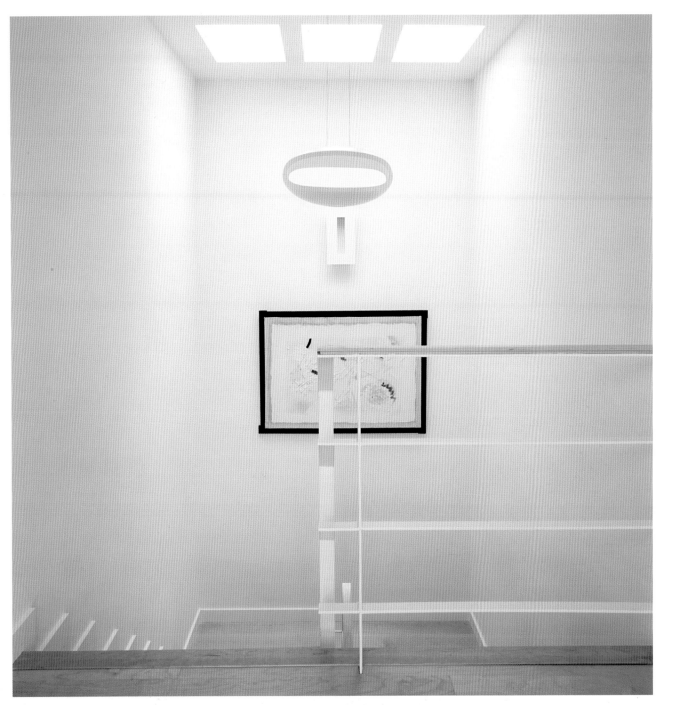

Staircases in passageways or in bright rooms should have transparent, thick acrylic or glass handrails to let light through and to integrate better into the room.

Treppen in sehr hellen Durchgangsbereichen oder Zimmern sollten durchsichtige Geländer aus Acryl oder sehr dickem Glas haben, damit sie das Licht durchlassen und sich besser in den Raum einfügen.

Les escaliers situés dans les lieux de passage ou dans les pièces très lumineuses devraient être équipés de balustrades transparentes, en acrylique ou en verre très épais, pour laisser passer la lumière et pour mieux s'intégrer à l'espace environnant.

Trappen in loopruimtes of zeer lichte kamers moeten heel dikke, doorschijnende leuningen – van acryl of glas – hebben, om het licht door te laten en beter te integreren in de ruimte.

When the stairs are wide and few, the steps are an excellent place to position decorative items. You can even place small candles or lamps on the steps.

Wenn die Treppe breit und kurz ist, sind die Stufen ein ausgezeichneter Platz für dekorative Gegenstände. Man kann sogar Kerzen oder kleine Lampen darauf stellen.

Si les escaliers sont larges et relativement bas, les marches constituent un excellent support pour les objets de décoration, tels de petites bougies ou des lampes.

Als de trap breed en kort is, zijn de treden een uitstekende plaats voor decoratieve voorwerpen. Er kunnen zelfs kleine kaarsen of lampen worden neergezet.

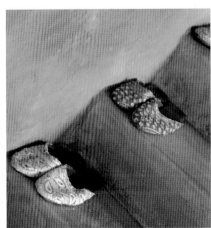

In environments with a mezzanine, put a ladder against the wall so as not to obstruct traffic. In this way it is stronger and safer.

In Räumen mit Zwischengeschoss bringen Sie die Treppe an der Wand an, damit die Zirkulation nicht behindert wird. Außerdem ist sie so stärker und sicherer.

Dans une pièce avec mezzanine, l'escalier peut être collé contre le mur pour éviter qu'il ne gêne la circulation, ce qui par ailleurs le rend aussi plus stable et plus sûr.

Plaats, in ruimtes met een tussenverdieping, de trap tegen de muur zodat deze geen sta-in-de-weg wordt. Dit is bovendien steviger en veiliger.

Stairwells offer numerous possibilities of use. A built-in bookshelf some 11 inches off the floor can be used as shelf, seat and storage.

Der Platz unter der Treppe bietet vielfältige Verwendungsmöglichkeiten. Ein in 30 cm Höhe eingebautes Bord fungiert als Regal, Sitzplatz und Stauraum.

Les escaliers offrent des espaces vides qui se prêtent à des usages multiples. Une bibliothèque en maçonnerie construite à 30 cm du sol devient une surface d'appoint, une banquette et un lieu de rangement.

De ruimte onder de trap biedt talrijke gebruiksmogelijkheden. Een gemetselde rand op 30 cm van de grond kan dienst doen als plank, zitplaats en opbergruimte.

When constructing a staircase, take into account the required slope and the measurement ratio of the steps so that they are easy to climb.

Beim Bau der Treppe berücksichtigen Sie die angemessene Neigung und die entsprechende Höhe der Stufen, damit man bequem hinaufgehen kann.

Lors de la construction d'un escalier, pour qu'il soit facile à monter, il faut que l'inclinaison soit correcte et les dimensions des marches proportionnées.

Houd bij het bouwen van de trap rekening met de geschikte klimlijn en de proportie van de afmetingen van de treden, zodat hij eenvoudig te beklimmen is.

The staircase must follow the style of the rest of the house. An easy way to do this is to use the same flooring on the steps as in the rest of the house.

Die Treppe sollte zum dem Stil des Hauses passen. Eine einfache Art, dies zu erreichen, ist die Stufen und Boden mit demselben Material zu belegen.

L'escalier doit s'intégrer au style de la maison. Pour ce faire, les marches peuvent être revêtues avec le même matériau utilisé pour le sol de la maison.

De trap moet worden gecombineerd met de stijl van de rest van de woning. Een eenvoudige manier om dat te bereiken is om in de treden dezelfde bekleding te gebruiken als op de vloer van de woning.

Ceiling lights on the landings must be dynamic when the stairs are very long. In this way, they also serve as a visual break.

Wenn die Treppen sehr hoch sind, müssen die Deckenlampen über den Treppenabsätzen groß genug sein. Dadurch wirken sie zudem als visueller Ruhepunkt.

Si l'"escalier est très large, la lampe de plafond décorant le palier doit être marquante. Elle servira ainsi de pause visuelle.

Plafondlampen in de overloop moeten overtuigend zijn als de trap heel lang is. Op deze manier doen ze ook dienst als visueel rustpunt.

The staircase passage is a good place to apply a dose
of bold color but similar to other areas of the house.

Der Treppenkorridor ist ein guter Ort für eine Dosis
auffallender Farbe, die allerdings auf die übrigen Flächen
des Hauses abgestimmt sein sollte.

Le couloir de l'escalier est un bon endroit pour appliquer
une touche de couleur vive, qui puisse toutefois
s'harmoniser avec les autres surfaces de la maison.

De gang van de trap is een goede plaats om een dosis
felle kleuren toe te passen, die wel in overeenkomst moet
zijn met de rest van de oppervlakken van het huis.

If the stairs are narrow and dark, paint the side walls white to create a feeling of spaciousness.

Wenn die Treppen schmal sind und aus dunklem Material bestehen, streichen Sie die Seitenwände weiß, um einen Eindruck von Weite zu vermitteln.

Si l'escalier est étroit et réalisé avec des matériaux sombres, il vaut mieux peindre les murs latéraux en blanc pour augmenter la sensation d'espace.

Verf, als de trap smal is en donker van kleur de zijwanden wit, zodat het geheel ruimer lijkt.

Improve safety on the stairs with spotlights on the roof, side panels and wall sconces. Install switches at the bottom and top of the staircase to be able to turn on and off the light from either point.

Erhöhen Sie die Sicherheit auf der Treppe durch in die Decke, in die Stufen oder seitlich eingebaute Strahler oder Wandlampen. Installieren Sie am Fuß und am Ende der Treppe Schalter, damit man das Licht an den jeweiligen Orten ein- und ausschalten kann.

La sécurité de votre escalier est renforcée par un éclairage au plafond, au niveau des marches ou latéral, ainsi que des appliques murales. Les interrupteurs situés au début et à la fin de la structure permettent d'allumer ou d'éteindre la lumière en toute sécurité.

Vergroot de veiligheid in de trap met in het plafond, traptreden of zijwanden ingebouwde spots en wandlampen. Installeer schakelaars onder en bovenaan de trap, zodat het licht op ieder moment kan worden aan en uitgedaan.

Single flight staircases can be located in the center
of the room to contribute to the layout of the space.

Eine einläufige, gerade Treppe kann in der Mitte des
Wohnzimmers errichtet werden und als Raumteiler dienen.

L'escalier droit à une seule volée peut occuper le
centre du salon, contribuant ainsi à distribuer l'espace
environnant.

Een trap met een rechte traparm moet in het midden van
de zitkamer worden geplaatst, om bij te dragen aan de
indeling van deze ruimte.

Slightly reduce the width of the stairs and make use
of the side against the wall to mount a shelf.

Machen Sie die Treppe etwas schmaler und stellen
Sie an der Wandseite ein Regal auf.

Réduisant légèrement la largeur de l'escalier, on obtient
un espace latéral accolé au mur où l'on peut installer
des étagères.

Maak de trap iets minder breed en benut de zijkant
tegen de muur om een boekenkast te monteren.

A cantilever spiral staircase is a great way to save space. It also adds a sculptural element to the space.

Eine Wendeltreppe ist eine ausgezeichnete Lösung, um Platz zu gewinnen. Außerdem bringt sie ein gestalterisches Element in den Raum.

L'escalier hélicoïdal à encorbellement constitue une excellente manière d'optimiser l'espace. Par ailleurs, il ajoute un élément sculptural à l'environnement.

Een zwevende wenteltrap is een uitstekende manier om ruimte te besparen. Het voegt bovendien een beeldhouw-element toe aan de ruimte.

Rugs in hallways should stand out in this transition space. It is therefore important to take time to find the model that best combines the tone and texture with the style of the house.

Die Teppiche in den Korridoren werten diesen Durchgangsbereich auf. Deshalb ist es wichtig, sich für die Suche nach einem Modell, das im Farbton und in der Textur am besten zum Stil des Hauses passt, Zeit zu nehmen.

Les tapis dans les couloirs enrichissent ces lieux de passage. Il est donc important de consacrer du temps à la recherche du modèle dont les couleurs et la matière s'adaptent le mieux au style de la maison.

Vloerkleden in de gangen leggen het accent op deze looproimte. Neem daarom de tijd om het model te zoeken dat qua kleur en textuur het beste past bij de stijl van de woning.

Corridors with skylights are ideal to place large plants. These potted ficus tree in large pots add a green touch to the house.

Flure mit Oberlicht sind ideal für die Aufstellung großer Pflanzen. Diese eingetopften Ficus-Bäume der Größe XXL bringen eine *green* Atmosphäre ins Haus.

Les couloirs avec verrière au plafond sont parfaits pour accueillir des plantes de grandes dimensions. Ces ficus en pots géants apportent une note verte à la maison.

Gangen met dakramen zijn ideaal om grote planten neer te zetten. Deze ficussen in XXL-formaat bloembakken geven de woning tevens een *groen* accent.

The staircase landing is not the only place you can hang a large format lamp. Place it in the middle of the slope at a height that does not get in the way.

Der Treppenabsatz ist nicht der einzige Ort, an dem man eine großformatige Lampe aufhängen kann. Hängen Sie die Lampe in die Mitte der Neigung in einer Höhe, die die Zirkulation nicht behindert.

Le palier de l'escalier n'est pas le seul endroit où l'on peut accrocher un lustre de grand format. Il peut être placé au centre de la pente à une hauteur qui ne gêne pas la circulation.

De overloop van de trap is niet de enige plaats waar een grote lamp kan worden opgehangen. Plaats deze halverwege de trap op een hoogte waardoor de doorgang niet belemmerd wordt.

Make use of outdoor passageways to put up a hammock and create a special corner in the courtyard.

Nutzen Sie die äußeren Korridore um eine Hängematte anzubringen und im Patio des Hauses eine besondere Nische zu schaffen.

Vous pouvez utiliser les couloirs extérieurs pour accrocher un hamac et créer ainsi un coin spécial dans la cour de la maison.

Gebruik de gangen buiten om een schommelbank te plaatsen en creëer zo een bijzonder plekje in de patio van de woning.

Very small patios can be converted into interior gardens and an important source of light for passageways. You only have to tear down the walls and replace them with windows.

Sehr kleine Patios kann man in Innengärten und in wichtige Lichtquellen für die Durchgangsbereiche verwandeln. Man muss nur die Wände abreißen und sie durch Glaswände ersetzen.

Les patios exigus peuvent devenir des jardins intérieurs et des sources de lumières importantes pour les zones de passage. Il faut juste abattre les murs en maçonnerie et les remplacer par des parois vitrées.

Kleine patio's kunnen worden omgebouwd tot binnentuinen en belangrijke lichtbronnen voor loopruimtes. U hoeft alleen de tussenmuren maar af te breken en deze te vervangen door glas.

An alternative to the typical indoor garden with plants is a Zen space made only with stones and sand.

Eine Alternative zum typischen Innenhofgarten mit Pflanzen bildet ein Zen-Raum, der nur aus Steinen und Sand besteht.

Vous pouvez profiter d'un décrochement dans le mur du couloir pour construire un canapé en maçonnerie.

Een alternatief voor een typische binnentuin met planten is een zen-inrichting met alleen stenen en zand.

Make a staircase stand out by painting the wall a color that contrasts with the rest of the room.

Heben Sie eine offene Treppe hervor, indem Sie die Stützwand in einer Farbe streichen, die mit dem übrigen Zimmer kontrastiert.

Vous pouvez mettre en valeur un escalier ouvert peignant le mur d'appui d'une couleur qui contraste avec le reste de la pièce.

Geef een open trap meer accent door de muur waartegen hij aanstaat in een kleur te schilderen die contrasteert met die van de rest van het vertrek.

Pictures help to make a transition wall between two rooms in the house stand out and can even connect the style of the spaces.

Bilder tragen dazu bei, eine Wand zwischen zwei Bereichen des Hauses hervorzuheben, und können sogar den Stil der beiden Bereiche verbinden.

Les tableaux contribuent à mettre en valeur une cloison de transition entre deux espaces et permettent aussi de relier les différents styles de la maison.

Schilderijen kunnen meehelpen om een muur die een overgang vormt tussen twee ruimtes van de woning te accentueren en kunnen zelfs de stijl van de ruimtes met elkaar verbinden.

The corridor leading to the bedroom can accommodate a wardrobe, hidden behind curtains that are both decorative and functional.

Im Flur, der zum Schlafzimmer führt, kann ein Kleiderschrank stehen, der hinter Vorhängen versteckt ist, die nicht nur nützlich, sondern auch dekorativ sind.

Le couloir conduisant à la chambre à coucher peut abriter une penderie ou un dressing, cachés derrière des rideaux aussi bien fonctionnels que décoratifs.

Op de gang naar een kamer kan een kledingkast worden neergezet, verborgen achter een gordijn dat, behalve functioneel, ook decoratief is.

Use a setback in the wall of the corridor to create a
built-in sofa.

Nutzen Sie eine Nische in der Flurwand, um ein Sofa
einzubauen.

Vous pouvez profiter d'un décrochement dans le mur
du couloir pour construire un canapé en maçonnerie.

Benut een terugspringing in de muur van de gang
om een gemetselde bank te maken.

Combine built-in step with other pieces of carpentry work and use them as drawers.

Kombinieren Sie eingebaute Stufen mit getischlerten Fächern und verwenden Sie sie als Schubfächer.

Les marches en maçonnerie alternées aux marches en bois deviennent des tiroirs.

Combineer gemetselde en houten traptreden en benut deze laatste als laden.

KITCHEN
KÜCHE
CUISINE
KEUKEN

If you enjoy cooking, install a fireplace for roasting and baking bread and pizza. It does not need to be a large space, just a good connection with the exterior.

Wenn Sie gerne kochen, bauen Sie einen Kaminofen zum Backen von Brot und Pizza ein. Man braucht keinen großen Raum, nur eine gute Verbindung nach draußen.

Si vous aimez cuisiner, vous pouvez installer une cheminée pour cuire votre pain et vos pizzas. Vous n'avez pas besoin de beaucoup d'espace, juste d'un bon lien avec l'extérieur.

Houdt u van koken, installeer dan een vuurhaard om brood en pizza in te bakken. Er is niet veel ruimte nodig, alleen een goede verbinding naar buiten toe.

Put appliances like the oven and the microwave on top of each other, located at the right height, to save space and convenience when working with them.

Bringen Sie Haushaltsgeräte wie Ofen und Mikrowelle übereinander in einer angemessenen Höhe an, um Platz zu gewinnen und bequem mit ihnen arbeiten zu können.

On peut superposer les éléments d'électroménagers, tels le four et le micro-ondes, à bonne hauteur, pour gagner de l'espace et qu'ils soient pratiques à utiliser.

Plaats huishoudelijke apparaten zoals de oven en de magnetron in een toren, op een geschikte hoogte, voor meer ruimte en comfort tijdens het koken.

Opt for furniture with deep drawers and organizers
that leave everything that you need in sight.

Entscheiden Sie sich für Schränke mit tiefen unterteilten
Schubladen, in denen alles, was man braucht, sichtbar ist.

Vous pouvez choisir des meubles avec des tiroirs profonds
et des rangements qui laissent voir tout ce dont vous avez
besoin.

Kies voor meubels met diepe laden met verdeelvakken
zodat alle benodigdheden in een oogopslag zichtbaar zijn.

A waste area below the worktop clears the work area more easily. Make use of the same space to organize cleaning products in a rack attached to the cupboard door.

Ein Bereich für die Abfälle unter der Arbeitsplatte erleichtert das Aufräumen des Arbeitsbereichs. Nutzen Sie denselben Platz, um die Putzmittel an einer an der Schranktür angebrachten Platte unterzubringen.

Un espace réservé aux déchets sous le plan de travail permet de le débarrasser plus facilement. On peut profiter de cette partie pour ranger les produits d'entretien dans un support monté contre la porte du meuble.

Afvalbakken onder het aanrecht zorgen ervoor dat de werkruimte gemakkelijk kan worden opgeruimd. Benut dezelfde plaats om schoonmaakmiddelen op te bergen in een rekje dat aan de kastdeur is bevestigd.

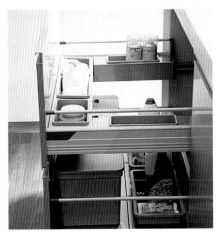

Easy-to-reach shelves are ideal for the most frequent
items. Store less frequently used items in lower drawers.

Die leicht erreichbaren Regale sind für die am häufigsten
gebrauchten Gegenstände geeignet. Bewahren Sie die
Dinge, die Sie seltener gebrauchen, in den unteren
Schubladen auf.

Les placards de rangement faciles à atteindre sont
destinés aux objets à usage fréquent. Les autres sont
réservés aux ustensiles les moins utilisés.

Planken waar men gemakkelijk bij kan zijn ideaal voor
de meestgebruikte voorwerpen. Bewaar de voorwerpen
die u het minst vaak gebruikt in de onderste lade.

Make use of empty spaces in the wall and mount a shelf for the dishes and glasses.

Nutzen Sie die freien Wandflächen und installieren Sie ein Regal für das Geschirr und die Gläser.

Les espaces vides du mur sont destinés aux étagères pour la vaisselle et les verres.

Benut lege ruimtes aan de muur en monteer een wandmeubel voor serviesgoed en glazen.

Use a shelf rack with wheels attached to the cabinet
to organize the pantry and provide easy access to all
products.

Verwenden Sie ein Regal auf Rollen neben dem Schrank
als Speiseschrank, um alle Produkte leicht zu erreichen.

Un espace de rangement coulissant entre les meubles est
une solution idéale pour ranger les produits alimentaires
et y accéder facilement.

Gebruik een uittrekbaar rek op wielen om de voorraadkast
te ordenen. Zo kunt u tevens gemakkelijk bij de producten
komen.

Save time by having items you use daily at hand. If they are classified by color or size, order is guaranteed.

Die Dinge des täglichen Gebrauchs bei der Hand zu haben spart Zeit; wenn sie außerdem nach Farben oder Größe geordnet sind, ist der Eindruck von Ordnung garantiert.

Avoir les objets à usage quotidien à portée de la main fait gagner du temps. Le classement par couleur ou par dimension assure un rangement très réussi.

Zorg dat u de voorwerpen die u dagelijks gebruikt bij de hand heeft; als u ze ook nog op kleur of maat sorteert ziet het er bovendien geordend uit.

To create order on open shelves group objects by shape or color. Inside cupboards the distribution of household goods does not have to be so fussy.

Offene Regale machen es erforderlich, dass die Gegenstände nach ähnlichen Formen oder Farben geordnet sind, um aufgeräumt zu wirken. Bringen sie die am wenigsten attraktiven Haushaltsgegenstände in den Schränken unter.

Les étagères ouvertes exigent que les objets soient rangés par forme ou par couleur pour donner la sensation d'ordre. Les ustensiles les moins attrayants sont distribués à l'intérieur des meubles.

Voor niet afgesloten wandmeubels moeten de voorwerpen op vorm of per kleur zijn gerangschikt, zodat het er opgeruimd uit ziet. Zet minder aantrekkelijke huisraad in de kasten.

If you have the space and a square-shaped kitchen, incorporate a kitchen island: it gives you extra working space and storage.

Wenn Sie Platz haben und die Küche einen quadratischen Grundriss hat, bauen Sie eine unabhängige Kochinsel ein: Dadurch gewinnen Sie einen zusätzlichen Arbeits- und Aufbewahrungsplatz.

Si vous disposez d'un espace cuisine carré, vous pouvez en profiter pour intégrer un îlot indépendant, qui augmente la surface du plan de travail et l'espace de rangement.

Heeft u voldoende ruimte en een keuken met vierkant oppervlak, aarzel dan niet om een onafhankelijk kookeiland te installeren: zo heeft u een groter werkoppervlak en meer opbergruimte.

Go for an island with a breakfast bar seating area so the family can gather in the kitchen while you are preparing the meal.

Wählen Sie eine Kochinsel mit Theke für Schnellmahlzeiten oder damit sich die Familie in der Küche versammeln kann, während Sie das Essen zubereiten.

Les îlots avec bar permettent de prendre des repas rapides. La famille peut aussi se réunir dans la cuisine pendant la préparation des plats.

Kies voor eilanden met bars voor een snelle maaltijd of als plaats waar het gezin bij elkaar kan zitten tijdens het bereiden van de maaltijd.

If the island does not have a bar, a ledge can be attached around the bar, at the same height or slightly lower and you will have an extra dining area.

Wenn die Kochinsel keine Theke hat, kann man eine Platte in derselben Höhe oder ein bisschen niedriger anbringen und so einen Essplatz gewinnen.

Si l'îlot n'a pas de bar, vous pouvez l'entourer d'une planche montée à la même hauteur ou à une hauteur légèrement inférieure. Vous gagnerez ainsi un espace supplémentaire destiné aux repas.

Als het eiland geen bar heeft, kan er rondom een oppervlak worden aangebouwd, op dezelfde hoogte of iets lager, zodat u ruimte heeft om te eten.

The refrigerator does not always have to be attached to the wall. Add a unit for the appliance to the central island.

Der Kühlschrank muss nicht immer an der Wand stehen. Stellen Sie neben der Mittelinsel ein Möbel auf, in dem Sie dieses Gerät unterbringen.

Le réfrigérateur ne doit pas toujours être collé au mur. Vous pouvez ajouter à l'îlot central un meuble destiné à accueillir cet appareil électroménager.

De koelkast hoeft niet altijd tegen de muur te staan. Verleng het centrale eiland met een meubelstuk om de koelkast in te zetten.

Replace one of the narrow drawers with a shelf that can serve as a working space.

Ersetzten Sie eine der schmalen Schubladen durch eine ausziehbare Platte, die als Beistelltisch dient.

Les petits tiroirs peuvent être remplacés par une planche coulissante faisant office de table d'appoint.

Vervang een of meerdere smalle laden door een uittrekbare plank die dienst kan doen als bijzettafel.

Instead of several small closets it is better to have a spacious bar and storage units under the sink. This will keep the upper half of the kitchen clutter-free.

Statt mehrerer kleiner Schränke ist es besser, über eine breite Theke und Schränke unter der Spüle zu verfügen. Auf diese Weise bleibt die obere Hälfte der Küche frei.

Au lieu de plusieurs petits placards, il vaut mieux disposer d'un plan très large et de meubles de rangement sous l'évier. De cette façon, on allège la partie supérieure de la cuisine.

In plaats van verschillende kleinere kasten is het beter om te beschikken over een ruime bar en lage meubels onder de gootsteen voor opbergruimte. Op die manier blijft de bovenste helft van de keuken vrij.

Add a touch of style to the kitchen with high designer stools at the bar.

Verleihen Sie der Küche mit hohen Designer-Hockern vor der Theke eine stilvolle Atmosphäre.

Ces tabourets de bar design apportent une touche de style à la cuisine.

Geef de keuken iets stijlvols met hoge design krukken aan de bar.

Install an elongated island in the American kitchen. It is a great way to separate the living room from this space with a fully functional object.

Bauen Sie eine verlängerte Insel vor die Amerikanische Küche. Das ist eine ausgezeichnete Art, diesen Bereich vom Wohnzimmer mit einem vollkommen funktionalen Möbelstück zu trennen.

Installer un îlot allongé devant la cuisine américaine est une excellente manière de séparer cet espace du salon grâce à un meuble complètement fonctionnel.

Installeer een langwerpig eiland tegenover een open keuken. Dat is een uitstekende manier om deze ruimte af te scheiden van de zitkamer met een uiterst functioneel ontwerp.

If you do not have much room for a small breakfast table in the kitchen, built-in benches save space and can be used to store objects.

Wenn Sie wenig Platz für das *office* (den Essplatz) in der Küche haben, sparen sie durch eingebaute Bänke Platz, und Sie können darin alle möglichen Dinge aufbewahren.

Si vous disposez d'un espace réduit pour la zone repas de la cuisine, les banquettes en maçonnerie permettent de gagner de la place et deviennent des espaces de rangement.

Beschikt u over beperkte ruimte voor een *office* in de keuken, dan krijgt u meer ruimte met gemetselde banken waarin u ook nog voorwerpen kunt opbergen.

Define the breakfast table with lighting and decoration that are different from the rest of the kitchen.

Grenzen Sie den Bereich des *office* (des Essplatzes) mit einer von der übrigen Küche unabhängigen Beleuchtung und Dekoration ab.

Vous pouvez délimiter la zone repas du reste de la cuisine par un éclairage et une décoration indépendants.

Baken de zone van de *office* af met verlichting en decoratie die onafhankelijk is van de rest van de woning.

The dining room should be designed with the same materials that prevail in this space so that it naturally integrates.

Der Essbereich sollte vorzugsweise aus denselben Materialien bestehen, die in der Küche vorherrschen, damit er sich natürlich einfügt.

Il est préférable que la table à manger et les chaises de la cuisine soient réalisées dans les mêmes matériaux que les autres éléments de cet espace pour qu'ils s'y intègrent naturellement.

De eethoek in de keuken moet bij voorkeur worden samengesteld uit de materialen die ook overheersen in deze ruimte voor een natuurlijke integratie.

Situate the dining room between the open kitchen and living room and you can intimately integrate these spaces that are used so often on a daily basis.

Installieren Sie den Essbereich zwischen Küche und Wohnzimmer, so können Sie diese Räume, die für das tägliche Leben so wichtig sind, verbinden.

Installer la salle à manger entre la cuisine ouverte et le salon permet de réunir ces espaces de la vie quotidienne si intimement reliés.

Plaats de eetkamer tussen de open keuken en de zitkamer in. Zo kunt u deze ruimtes die zo zijn verbonden met het dagelijkse leven integreren.

Place the dinner table right next to the island and you will have an additional surface to place dishes, trays, bottles and bread baskets while eating.

Platzieren Sie den Esstisch dicht an die Insel und gewinnen Sie so einen zusätzliche Fläche zum Abstellen von Schüsseln, Flaschen und Brotkörben während des Essens.

Coller la table à manger à l'îlot de la cuisine augmente la surface servant de support aux plats, plateaux, bouteilles et corbeilles à pain pendant les repas.

Zet de eettafel tegen het eiland aan. Zo verkrijgt u extra ruimte om schalen, bladen, flessen en broodmanden op te zetten tijdens de maaltijd.

The kitchen dining room should have enough room to move comfortably, with a suitable size table and chairs that fit in easily.

Der Essbereich der Küche sollte mit einem Tisch von entsprechender Größe und Stühlen, die sich leicht stapeln lassen, genügend Bewegungsfreiheit bieten.

La table à manger et les chaises de la cuisine doivent bien évidemment aller ensemble et laisser la place suffisante pour bouger aisément.

De eethoek van de keuken moet voldoende ruimte overlaten zodat men zich comfortabel kan bewegen, met een tafel van geschikte afmetingen en stoelen die eenvoudig kunnen worden aangeschoven.

Install good lighting in particular above the worktop. Besides being very useful when handling food, light adds warmth to the kitchen, as opposed to cold lighting on the ceiling.

Beleuchten Sie besonders die Arbeitsfläche. Außer, dass diese Beleuchtung bei der Handhabung der Lebensmittel sehr nützlich ist, bringt sie im Gegensatz zu der kalten Deckenbeleuchtung Wärme in die Küche.

Un bon éclairage du plan de travail aide à mieux manipuler les aliments et réchauffe l'atmosphère de la cuisine, contrairement à l'éclairage froid du plafond.

Zorg vooral voor een goede verlichting van het aanrecht. Behalve dat dat nuttig is bij het bereiden van het eten, geeft het licht warmte in de keuken, tegenover de koele plafondverlichting.

A rustic kitchen can become a very welcoming and practical space by combining wood and steel, simple, solid pieces of furniture and natural fiber stools.

Eine rustikale Küche kann durch die Kombination von Holz und Stahl, einfachen und stabilen Möbeln und Hockern aus Naturfasern sowohl gemütlich als auch praktisch sein.

L'association du bois et de l'acier, de meubles simples et solides et de tabourets en fibre naturelle donne à la cuisine rustique un aspect accueillant et pratique.

Een landelijke keuken kan worden omgebouwd tot een gezellige en praktische ruimte met de combinatie hout en staal, eenvoudige en solide meubels en krukken van natuurvezel.

Opt for skylights in the ceiling or upper part of the wall
to flood the kitchen with natural light.

Verwenden Sie Oberlichter in der Decke oder im oberen
Teil der Wände, um natürliches Licht in die Küche zu
lassen.

Des ouvertures au plafond ou dans la partie supérieure
des murs inondent la cuisine de lumière naturelle.

Neem uw toevlucht tot dakramen in het plafond of
bovenaan de muren om uw keuken in het daglicht te zetten.

Do not neglect the decor of the dining area just because it is incorporated into the kitchen. Rugs can also be used in this space. Just leave a free strip on the floor in front of the worktop.

Vernachlässigen Sie die Dekoration des Essbereiches nicht, weil er in die Küche integriert ist. Teppiche sind auch für diesen Raum geeignet. Lassen Sie nur einen freien Gang auf dem Boden vor der Arbeitsfläche.

La décoration de la salle à manger ne doit pas être négligée sous prétexte qu'elle se trouve dans l'espace de la cuisine. Les tapis ont aussi leur importance. Il faut juste laisser un couloir libre devant le plan de travail.

Veronachtzaam de decoratie van de eetkamer niet omdat deze in de keuken ligt. Ook vloerkleden zijn geschikt voor deze ruimte. Laat alleen een strook open op de grond voor het aanrecht.

Use lamps to emphasize the definition of the breakfast table in the kitchen and provide good lighting to the area where you eat.

Verwenden Sie die Lampen, um den Bereich des *office* in der Küche abzugrenzen und den Essplatz gut zu beleuchten.

Vous pouvez utiliser les lampes pour mieux délimiter l'espace de la zone repas dans la cuisine et l'éclairer convenablement.

Maak gebruik van lampen om de afbakening van de *office* in de keuken te versterken en zorg voor een goede verlichting van de eethoek.

Steam in the kitchen tends to permeate the furnishings.
Choose steel or acrylic lamps as they are easier to clean.

Die Küchendämpfe neigen dazu, sich im Mobiliar
festzusetzen. Wählen Sie Lampen aus Stahl oder
Metacrylat, weil diese leichter zu säubern sind.

Les vapeurs de la cuisine tendent à imprégner le mobilier :
les lampes en acier ou en méthacrylate sont plus faciles
à nettoyer.

Keukendampen kunnen in het meubilair impregneren.
Kies voor stalen of methacrylaat lampen, omdat die
eenvoudiger kunnen worden schoongemaakt.

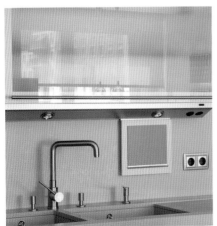

The kitchen must combine different types of lighting, aesthetics and safety. A single lamp on the ceiling casts a shadow of the cook on the hob, which remains visible.

In der Küche braucht man aus ästhetischen und Sicherheitsgründen verschiedene Arten von Beleuchtung. Eine einzelne Lampe an der Decke wirft den Schatten desjenigen, der kocht, auf die Arbeitsfläche und behindert damit die Sicht.

La cuisine doit posséder différents types d'éclairage, pour des raisons esthétiques et de sécurité. Une seule lampe au plafond projette l'ombre de la personne qui cuisine sur le plan de travail, diminuant ainsi la visibilité.

In de keuken moeten uit esthetische en veiligheidsoverwegingen verschillende soorten verlichting worden gecombineerd. Een enkele plafondlamp projecteert de schaduw van degene die kookt op het werkblad en neemt het licht weg.

New compact quartz and resin materials for the worktop have a nice texture to the touch, there are no joints and are very resistant to wear and scratches.

Die neuen kompakten Materialien für die Arbeitsflächen aus Quarz und Harzen fühlen sich angenehm an, haben keine Fugen und sind sehr widerstandsfähig gegenüber Abnutzung und Kratzern.

Les nouveaux matériaux compacts à base de quartz et de résines utilisés pour les plans de travail sont agréables au toucher, n'ont pas de jointures et sont très résistants à l'usure et aux égratignures.

Nieuwe compacte materialen van kwarts en hars voor het werkblad voelen aangenaam aan, hebben geen naden en zijn bestendig tegen slijtage en krassen.

Black has taken over the modern and stylish kitchens. But the area where food is handled and cooked should be in a contrasting color, preferably white.

Schwarz hat sich der modernen, eleganten Küchen bemächtigt. Aber die Bereiche für die Verarbeitung und das Kochen von Lebensmitteln sollten in einer kontrastierenden Farbe, vorzugsweise weiß, gehalten sein.

Le noir a pris possession des cuisines modernes et élégantes. Toutefois, les plans de travail et de cuisson doivent avoir une couleur qui se détache de l'ensemble, de préférence le blanc.

Zwart is toonaangevend in moderne en elegante keukens. Maar de plaats waar men het eten bereikt en kookt moet een contrasterende kleur hebben, bij voorkeur wit.

Delimit the wall above the worktop with a special cladding such as tiles, plastic paint, plastic slats or imitation wood to protect it from splashes.

Beschichten Sie die Wand über der Arbeitsfläche mit einer Spezialverkleidung wie Fliesen, Kunststoff-Anstrich oder Plastiklamellen aus Holzimitat, um sie gegen Spritzer zu schützen.

On peut délimiter le mur au-dessus du plan de travail avec un revêtement spécial – carrelage, peinture imperméable ou film plastifié imitant le bois – pour le protéger des éclaboussures.

Begrens de wand boven het aanrecht met een speciale bekleding zoals tegels, synthetische muurverf of plastic houtimitatie platen die bestand zijn tegen spatten.

Modern appliances have abandoned the traditional white and steel colors to incorporate beautiful colors that add a special touch to the kitchen.

Die modernen elektrischen Haushaltsgeräte unterwerfen sich nicht mehr der Diktatur von Weiß und Stahl. Es gibt sie heute in attraktiven Farben, die der Küche eine besondere Note verleihen.

Les appareils électroménagers modernes ont quitté la dictature du blanc et de l'acier pour revêtir des couleurs vives apportant une touche spéciale à la cuisine.

De moderne huishoudelijke apparaten zijn allang niet meer alleen wit en van staal, maar hebben tegenwoordig aantrekkelijke kleuren die de keuken een speciaal accent geven.

Use steel coatings and worktops to create an industrial environment. It is very easy to clean but remember it also scratches very easily.

Verwenden Sie Verkleidungen und Arbeitsflächen aus Stahl, um eine industrielle Atmosphäre zu schaffen. Sie sind sehr leicht zu reinigen, aber denken Sie daran, dass sie leicht verkratzen.

Les revêtements et les plans de travail en acier créent une ambiance industrielle : ils sont très simples à nettoyer mais ils se rayent facilement.

Gebruik bekledingen en stalen werkbladen voor een industriële sfeer. Hoewel dat eenvoudig schoon te maken is, moet u wel uitkijken voor krassen.

The stone coverings are usually very porous and it is then very difficult to remove grease stains. For this reason a special treatment should be applied to seal the pores.

Die Täfelungen aus Stein sind normalerweise sehr porös, und es ist später sehr schwierig, Fettflecken zu entfernen. Deshalb sollte man sie zuvor mit einem Spezialmittel behandeln, um die Poren zu versiegeln.

Les revêtements en pierre sont généralement très poreux et il est difficile d'enlever les taches de graisse à posteriori. Il vaut donc mieux les traiter préalablement pour garantir leur étanchéité.

Stenen bekledingen kunnen erg poreus zijn en vlekken zijn daarom moeilijk te verwijderen. Daarom is het raadzaam om een speciale behandeling uit te voeren, om de poriën af te dichten.

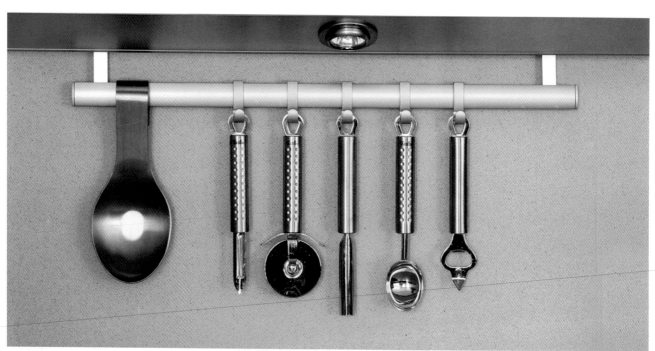

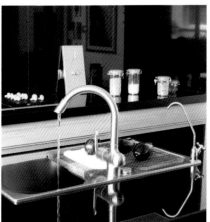

Only install a high spout faucet if the sink is large, otherwise it will continuously splash the worktop. If you don't have much space, the faucet should be attached to the wall.

Installieren Sie nur dann einen Wasserhahn mit hohem Wasserstrahl, wenn das Spülbecken groß ist, sonst gibt es immer Spritzer auf der Arbeitsfläche. Wenn Sie sehr wenig Platz haben, ist ein Wasserhahn, der direkt aus der Wand kommt, ideal.

Le robinet à long col n'est indiqué que si l'évier est grand, sinon le plan de travail présentera toujours des éclaboussures. Si vous disposez de très peu de place, le robinet sortant directement du mur est la meilleure solution.

Installeer uitsluitend een kraan met hoge uitloop als de gootsteen groot is, anders krijgt u altijd spatten op het aanrecht. Heeft u weinig ruimte, dan is een kraan die rechtstreeks uit de muur komt een uitkomst.

Some worktop models are specially designed as troughs that bring water directly to the sink and therefore pools of water do not form, or metal strips that serve as a trivet.

Manche Arbeitsplattenmodelle haben ein besonderes Design, wie z.B. Metall-Leisten in der Art von Untersetzern oder Abflussrinnen, die das Wasser direkt in das Spülbecken leiten und die Pfützen verschwinden lassen.

Certains modèles de plan de travail ont un design particulier, comme les petites canalisations conduisant l'eau directement à l'évier et faisant disparaître les résidus liquides ou les barres métalliques servant de dessous-de-plat.

Sommige modellen werkbladen hebben een speciaal ontwerp, zoals gootjes die het water rechtstreeks naar de gootsteen leiden, zodat er geen plasjes ontstaan, of metalen stroken die dienst doen als placemats.

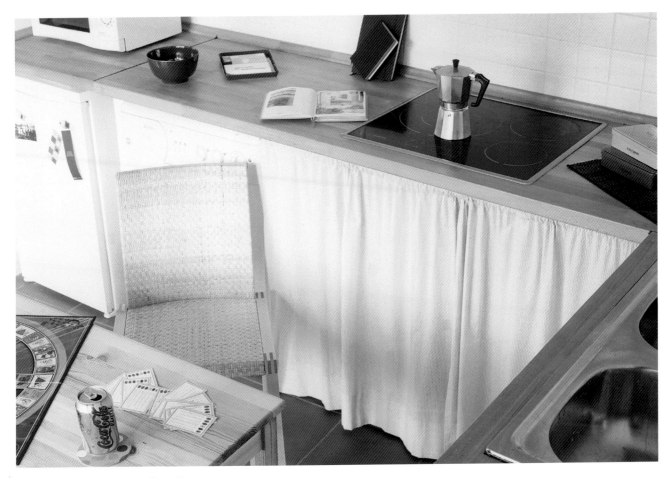

The curtains below the worktop are still a good resource to keep shelves and their contents out of sight. Opt for white or a solid color, without prints, to give the kitchen a modern look.

Vorhänge unter der Arbeitsfläche sind immer noch ein gutes Mittel, Regale und deren Inhalt zu verbergen. Umso besser, wenn sie weiß oder einfarbig, und ungemustert sind, damit sie modern wirken.

Les rideaux en bas de l'évier sont toujours un bon moyen pour cacher les étagères et leur contenu. Idéalement, elles sont blanches ou d'une couleur unie, sans dessins imprimés, ce qui leur confère un air moderne.

Gordijnen onder het aanrecht zijn nog steeds een handig hulpmiddel om planken en de inhoud daarvan te verbergen. Wit of een effen kleur, zonder opdruk, zijn de beste keuze, voor een moderne aanblik.

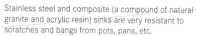

Stainless steel and composite (a compound of natural granite and acrylic resin) sinks are very resistant to scratches and bangs from pots, pans, etc.

Spülbecken aus rostfreiem Stahl und *composite* (eine Kombination aus Naturgranit und Acrylharz) sind sehr widerstandsfähig gegen Kratzer und durch Pfannen, Töpfe, usw. verursachte Stöße.

Les éviers en acier inoxydables et en composite (un mélange de granit naturel et de résine acrylique) sont très résistants aux rayures et aux coups de poêle, de casserole, etc.

Gootstenen van roestvrij staal en *composite* (een samenstelling van natuurlijk graniet en kunsthars) zijn goed bestand tegen krassen en klappen van koekenpannen, grote pannen, etc.

Ceramic materials for flooring, including different types of sandstone and clay, are all very durable, easy to clean and available in a wide range of finishes and colors.

Die verschiedenen Keramikmaterialien für den Boden von Steingut bis gebranntem Ton sind alle sehr hart, leicht zu reinigen und in vielen unterschiedlichen Ausführungen und Farben erhältlich.

Les carrelages pour le sol – des différents types de grès à la terre cuite – sont tous très résistants, faciles à nettoyer et ils présentent une large gamme de finitions et de couleurs.

Keramiek materialen voor de vloer, vanaf verschillende soorten aardewerk tot gebakken klei, zijn alle zeer hard, eenvoudig schoon te maken en met een waaier aan afwerkingen en kleuren.

Although, in theory, wood is not the best choice for kitchen flooring, thanks to modern pore sealing treatments, extremely hard-wearing floors are available that give warmth to this space.

Auch wenn Holz grundsätzlich nicht der beste Bodenbelag für eine Küche ist, gibt es dank der modernen Versiegelungstechniken sehr widerstandsfähige Böden, die diesem Raum Wärme verleihen.

Même si, à l'origine, le bois n'est pas le revêtement le plus adapté au sol de la cuisine, il apporte de la chaleur à cette pièce. Ils en existent actuellement de très résistants, grâce à des traitements modernes qui augmentent leur étanchéité.

Hoewel een houten vloer in principe niet geschikt is voor de keuken, bestaan er dankzij de moderne behandelingen waarmee de poriën worden afgedicht zeer bestendige vloeren die deze ruimte de nodige warmte geven.

Opt for textures and colors capable of hiding stains and that are not very bright, as they can be very slippery.

Entscheiden Sie sich für Texturen und Farben, auf denen man die Flecken nicht so leicht sieht, und die nicht sehr glänzen, da sie sonst rutschig sind.

On peut choisir des matériaux et des couleurs permettant de dissimuler les taches et qui ne soient pas très brillants, même s'ils sont glissants.

Kies voor texturen en kleuren waarop vlekken niet goed te zien zijn en die niet glanzend zijn, om uitglijden te voorkomen.

To avoid having to replace a porous kitchen floor, install a metal plate on the floor around the food handling area, which is the area where most dirt accumulates.

Damit Sie nicht den porösen Boden der Küche erneuern müssen, installieren Sie um den Bereich herum, in dem die Lebensmittel verarbeitet werden, eine Metallbahn auf dem Boden, da dort am meisten Schmutz entsteht.

Pour ne pas remplacer le revêtement poreux du sol de la cuisine, on installe une plaque métallique autour de la partie la plus salissante, qui est celle où l'on manipule les aliments.

Installeer, om de poreuze vloer van de keuken niet te hoeven vervangen, een metalen plaat op de grond rond de zone waar met eten gewerkt wordt en die het snelste vuil wordt.

In small kitchens, use sliding doors or walls and glass partitions to save space and allow sufficient light through.

In kleinen Küchen installieren Sie Schiebetüren oder Zwischenwände mit Glas, um Platz zu sparen und Licht einzulassen.

Si la cuisine est petite, les portes coulissantes ou les cloisons en verre permettent d'optimiser l'espace et de laisser entrer la lumière.

Neem in kleine keukens uw toevlucht tot schuifpuien of glazen tussenmuurtjes om ruimte te besparen en licht te laten invallen.

Create a vibrant, stunning kitchen with vinyl on the wall with the image of a market stall. The resistance of this material to steam and heat guarantees it to be long-lasting.

Schaffen Sie eine überraschende und beschwingte Küche mit einer Vinyltapete, die einen Marktstand vortäuscht. Die Resistenz dieses Materials gegen Dämpfe und Hitze garantiert eine lange Lebensdauer.

Ce vinyle décoratif mural représentant un étalage du marché crée un effet de surprise très réussi dans cette cuisine. La résistance de ces stickers à la vapeur et à la chaleur leur assure une longue durée de vie.

Creëer een verrassende en levendige keuken met vinyl op de muren waarop een marktkraam is afgebeeld. De bestendigheid van dit materiaal tegen stoom en warmte garandeert een lange levensduur.

Separate the kitchen from the dining room with a glass expanse with motifs associated with the kitchen such as recipes or images of accessories.

Trennen Sie die Küche vom Essplatz mit einer Glasscheibe, die mit Küchenmotiven wie Rezepten oder Zeichnungen von Küchengeräten dekoriert ist, ab.

La cuisine peut être séparée de la salle à manger par une cloison en verre ornée de motifs liés à la cuisine, tels des recettes ou des dessins d'accessoires.

Scheid de keuken van de eetkamer af door glas met motieven die te maken hebben met de keuken, zoals recepten of tekeningen van accessoires.

Even if the kitchen is very small, there's always room for a decorative detail that makes it a pleasant space. Use drawings on the wall or an original, eye-catching clock.

Auch wenn die Küche sehr klein ist, gibt es immer Platz für ein dekoratives Detail, das sie in einen gemütlichen Raum verwandelt. Dekorieren Sie die Wand mit graphischen Motiven oder einer originellen, auffallenden Uhr.

Même si la cuisine est très petite, il y a toujours de la place pour un détail décoratif : des dessins sur le mur ou une pendule originale constituent des solutions intéressantes.

Ook al is de keuken klein, er is altijd wel een plekje voor een decoratief detail om er een aangename ruimte van te maken. Denk aan muurtekeningen of een originele, opvallende klok.

CHILDREN'S BEDROOM

KINDERZIMMER

CHAMBRE D'ENFANT

KINDERKAMER

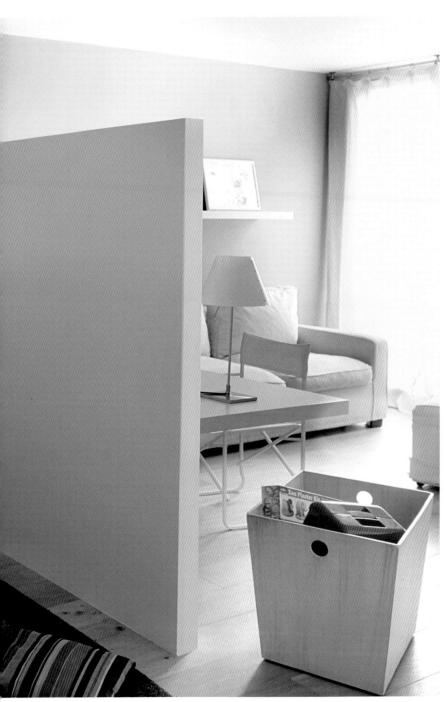

Place a partition in the middle of the room that serves as a support for one of the beds and separates the rest area from the play area.

Bringen Sie in der Zimmermitte eine Trennwand an, die als Stützwand für eins der Betten dient und den Schlaf- vom Spielbereich trennt.

La cloison au centre de la pièce sert de support à l'un des lits et sépare le coin repos du coin jeu.

Plaats een tussenmuur midden in de kamer als steun voor een van de bedden en scheid het slaapgedeelte af van het speelgedeelte.

A bunk bed with a zigzag structure provides storage capacity, as the high bed rests on a closet.

Mit einem zickzackförmig angebrachten Etagenbett gewinnt man Stauraum, da das Hochbett auf einem Schrank aufliegt.

Les lits superposés décalés augmentent la capacité de rangement, car le lit en haut repose sur une armoire.

Met een zig-zag stapelbed heeft u meer opbergruimte, aangezien het bovenste bed op een kledingkast steunt.

Take advantage of an almost square room with two beds at an angle or facing each other and another higher bed accessed via a ladder.

Nutzen Sie ein Zimmer mit fast quadratischem Grundriss aus, und stellen Sie zwei Betten rechtwinklig zueinander oder gegenüber auf und installieren Sie ein weiteres, das man mit einer Leiter erreicht, sehr hoch darüber.

On peut tirer parti d'une chambre presque carrée avec deux lits d'angle ou côte à côte et un autre placé au-dessus, auquel on accède par une échelle.

Benut een slaapmaker met vierkant grondplan optimaal met twee bedden in een hoek of tegenover elkaar en een bed daarboven, met een trap.

Use the space under the bed to store boxes and drawers with clothes and toys.

Nutzen Sie den Platz unter dem Bett aus, um Kästen und Schubladen mit Wäsche oder Spielzeug unterzubringen.

L'espace sous le lit peut accueillir des boîtes et des tiroirs pour ranger des vêtements et des jouets.

Benut de ruimte onder het bed voor laden om kleding of speelgoed in te bewaren.

Personalize the children's bedroom with decorative objects that also help maintain order, such as this coat rack reminiscent of a school rack.

Geben Sie dem Kinderzimmer eine persönliche Note mit dekorativen Objekten, die zudem helfen, Ordnung zu halten, wie dieser Kleiderständer, der an diejenigen erinnert, die es in der Schule gibt.

La chambre d'enfant peut être personnalisée avec des objets de décoration qui servent aussi de rangement, comme ce porte-manteau rappelant l'école.

Maak de kinderkamer persoonlijk met decoratieve voorwerpen zodat die er bovendien opgeruimder uitziet, zoals deze kapstok die doet denken aan die van school.

So that the wallpaper print is not too overwhelming, cover three quarters of the area and leave the top part white.

Damit das Tapetenmuster nicht erdrückend wirkt, tapezieren Sie drei Viertel der Fläche und lassen Sie den oberen Teil weiß.

Pour ne pas se lasser du papier peint, il suffit de ne couvrir que trois quarts de la surface et de laisser la partie supérieure en blanc.

Behang hoeft niet meer overladen te zijn als u drie vierde van het oppervlak behangt en de bovenkant wit laat.

If there is space in the master bedroom for the baby's crib, use a chest of drawers at the foot of the large bed to separate the spaces.

Wenn es im Elternschlafzimmer Platz für eine Wiege gibt, stellen Sie eine Kommode am Fußende des Doppelbetts auf, um den Raum zu unterteilen.

Si dans la chambre à coucher principale il y a de la place pour le berceau du bébé, on peut séparer les espaces avec une commode à roulette installée au pied du grand lit.

Is er voldoende ruimte in de slaapkamer voor een wieg, gebruik dan een commode aan de voet van het grote bed om de ruimtes te scheiden.

Maintain visual continuity using colors from the same family (such as cool colors, blue, green, violet or cyan). This creates an environment that conveys serenity, suitable for children's rooms.

Erhalten Sie das einheitliche Aussehen durch Farben derselben Familie (wie kalte Farben, Blau, Grün, Violett oder Türkis). Auf diese Weise wird eine ruhige Atmosphäre geschaffen, die für Kinderzimmer sehr geeignet ist.

Maintenir la continuité visuelle en utilisant des couleurs de la même famille – comme des couleurs froides, le bleu, le vert, le violet ou le cyan – crée une atmosphère sereine très adaptée aux chambres d'enfant.

Behoud de visuele continuïteit door gebruik te maken van kleuren van dezelfde familie (zoals koude kleuren, blauw, groen, violet of cyaan). Op die manier creëert u een ruimte die rust uitstraalt, zeer geschikt voor kinderkamers.

Even though the bedroom is large, leave as much space as possible to let children play, jump and run. Do not cram it with furniture.

Auch wenn das Zimmer groß ist, lassen Sie so viel Platz wie möglich frei, damit die Kinder spielen, springen und rennen können. Überladen Sie es nicht mit Möbeln.

Même si la chambre est grande, il faut laisser le plus d'espace possible pour que les enfants jouent, sautent et courent, sans la remplir de meubles.

Laat, ook bij grote slaapkamers, zo veel mogelijk ruimte leeg zodat kinderen er kunnen spelen, springen en rennen. Zet de slaapkamer niet vol met meubels.

Boxes or baskets are very practical for storing toys in a quick and easy manner, and to get kids used to tidying up when they finish playing.

Kästen oder Körbe sind sehr praktisch, um schnell und einfach Spielzeuge aufzubewahren, und die Kinder daran zu gewöhnen, die Sachen aufzuräumen, wenn sie mit dem Spielen aufgehört haben.

Les boîtes ou les paniers sont très pratiques pour ranger de manière facile et rapide les jouets et habituer les enfants à remettre les affaires à leur place quand ils ont terminé de jouer.

Dozen of manden zijn praktisch om speelgoed snel op te bergen en om kinderen te leren om na het spelen hun speelgoed op te ruimen.

Decorate a girl's bedroom with a border on the wall
made of cardboard cutouts that she may even draw.

Dekorieren Sie das Mädchenzimmer mit einem
Wandschutz, der aus ausgeschnittenen Kartonfiguren
besteht, die das Kind sogar selbst zeichnen kann.

Une chambre de fille peut être décorée avec une frise
composée d'images découpées en carton, éventuellement
dessinées par elle-même.

Versier de meisjeskamer met een strook aan de muur
waaraan uit karton geknipte figuren worden gehangen,
die zij ook zelf kan tekenen.

Choose a large wardrobe with simple lines where you can also store bed clothes. You will be able to use it for many years.

Wählen Sie einen Schrank mit klaren Linien und großem Fassungsvermögen, in dem man auch die Bettwäsche unterbringen kann. Außerdem kann man ihn viele Jahre lang gebrauchen.

Une grande armoire aux lignes simples peut contenir aussi le linge de lit. En plus, elle pourra être utilisée pendant des années.

Kies een kast met eenvoudige lijnen en grote capaciteit, zodat u er ook beddengoed in kwijt kunt. U kunt de kast dan nog vele jaren gebruiken.

In large, shared bedrooms divide the space with partitions to define the sleeping area from the study and play areas.

In sehr großen Zimmern, die sich die Kinder teilen, trennen Sie den Raum durch Trennwände, um den Schlafbereich von dem Lern- und Spielbereich zu trennen.

Vous pouvez distribuer l'espace des chambres partagées et très grandes à l'aide de cloisons qui délimitent le coin repos, l'espace de travail et le coin jeu.

In gedeelde en heel grote slaapkamers kunt u de ruimte indelen met tussenschotten om het slaapgedeelte van het studeer- en speelgedeelte af te scheiden.

Purchase a large container with a lid and wheels for storing toys, bedding and books Once closed it can also be used as a bench or bedside table.

Stellen Sie einen großen Behälter mit Deckel und Rädern auf, um Spielzeug, Bettwäsche oder Bücher darin aufzubewahren. Wenn er geschlossen ist, kann er auch als Bank oder Nachttisch benutzt werden.

Ce caisson à roulettes avec couvercle peut contenir des jouets, du linge de lit ou des livres. Une fois fermé, il peut aussi être utilisé comme banquette ou comme table de nuit.

Installeer een grote bak met deksel en wieltjes om speelgoed, beddengoed of boeken in te bewaren. Afgesloten kan hij ook gebruikt worden als bank of nachtkastje.

Choose wallpaper that is both decorative and educational. How about a world map for the child's bedroom walls?

Wählen Sie eine Tapete, die gleichzeitig lehrreich und dekorativ ist. Wie wäre es mit einer Weltkarte an den Wänden des Kinderzimmers?

Ce papier peint est à la fois décoratif et instructif. Pourquoi n'amèneriez-vous pas la mappemonde sur les murs de la chambre d'enfant ?

Kies voor behang dat tegelijkertijd decoratief als leerzaam is. Wat te denken van een wereldkaart op de muren van de kinderkamer?

BEDROOM

SCHLAFZIMMER

CHAMBRE À COUCHER

SLAAPKAMER

Choose transparent bedside tables to create a feeling of more space beside the bed. If they are nest tables, you can use them for breakfast.

Wählen Sie durchsichtige Nachttischchen, um den Eindruck von mehr Platz neben dem Bett zu schaffen. Wenn Sie zudem ineinanderpassen, können Sie sie für das Frühstück benutzen.

Les tables de nuit transparentes augmentent la sensation d'espace sur les côtés du lit. Si elles ont une niche, elles peuvent être utilisées aussi pour le petit déjeuner.

Kies doorschijnende nachtkastjes, zodat de ruimte aan weerszijden van het bed groter lijkt. Tafeltjes die in elkaar kunnen worden geschoven zijn zelfs te gebruiken om te ontbijten.

Discard traditional bedside tables and place a colorful living room side table to give the room a personal touch.

Lassen Sie die traditionellen Nachttische außer Acht, und stellen Sie einen Wohnzimmer-Beistelltisch in einer auffallenden Farbe neben das Bett, um dem Schlafzimmer eine persönliche Note zu geben.

Une table d'appoint du salon aux couleurs vives peut remplacer la table de nuit traditionnelle et apporter à la chambre à coucher une touche personnelle.

Verwerp traditionele nachtkastjes en plaats een bijzettafel in een opvallende kleur naast het bed, om de slaapkamer een persoonlijk tintje te geven.

A square shelf hanging over the side of the bed is a bedside table that takes up very little space and is visually very light.

Ein freischwebendes quadratisches Regalbrett an der Bettseite dient als Nachttisch, der sehr wenig Platz einnimmt und sehr leicht aussieht.

Une planche carrée saillante montée à côté du lit devient une table de nuit qui occupe très peu de place et apporte visuellement une grande légèreté.

Een zwevende vierkante plank naast het bed is een nachtkastje dat weinig ruimte inneemt en tegelijkertijd visueel licht is.

If the space is narrow or to gain more support surface, fit a shelf on the wall parallel to the bed, so that it can be used as a bedside table.

Wenn der Raum sehr eng ist, oder um mehr Abstellfläche zu gewinnen, bringen Sie ein Regalbrett als Nachttisch an der Wand an, die parallel zum Bett verläuft.

Par manque d'espace ou pour augmenter la surface à votre disposition, vous pouvez installer une étagère sur le mur parallèle au lit, faisant office de table de nuit.

Installeer, hetzij omdat de ruimte smal is of om meer steunoppervlak te krijgen, een plank aan de wand parallel aan het bed, zodat die dienst kan doen als nachtkastje.

Build a headboard that serves as a shelf and that also has a shelf with cover that, when opened, becomes a nightstand.

Lassen Sie ein Kopfteil für das Bett bauen, das als Regal dient und in das ein Klappbrett eingebaut ist, das sich aufgeklappt in einen Nachttisch verwandelt.

Vous pouvez vous faire construire une tête de lit avec bibliothèque, pouvant accueillir une tablette rabattable qui, une fois ouverte, devient une table de nuit.

Laat een hoofdeinde maken dat ook fungeert als plank en dat groot genoeg is voor een uitstekende rand met afdekking die, als hij geopend wordt, wordt omgevormd tot een nachtkastje.

Replace the traditional bedside table for an old suitcase or trunk. The advantage is that you can store other seasonal clothing or blankets inside.

Ersetzten Sie den traditionellen Nachttisch durch einen alten Koffer oder eine Truhe. Das hat den Vorteil, dass man darin Kleidung für andere Jahreszeiten oder Decken aufbewahren kann.

Une vieille valise ou une malle peut remplacer la table de nuit traditionnelle : elle présente l'avantage de contenir des vêtements d'une autre saison ou des couvertures.

Vervang het traditionele tafeltje door een oude koffer of hutkoffer. Bijkomend voordeel is dat u er kleding van andere seizoenen of dekens in kunt opbergen.

If there is a setback in the wall, create a built-in baseboard-headboard that serves as a shelf, perfect to support the table lamp.

Wenn sich eine Nische in der Wand befindet, bauen Sie einen Sockel, der als Ablage dient und einen idealen Platz für die Nachtischlampe bietet.

Si le mur présente un décrochement, une tête de lit en maçonnerie fait office d'étagère et est idéale pour poser des lampes de table.

Als de muur een inspringend gedeelte heeft, creëer dan een gemetselde sokkel-hoofdeinde die dienst doet als schap, ideaal om de tafellamp op te zetten.

If you do not have a bedside table or it is very small, install a lighting fixture that hangs from the ceiling close to the height of the bed.

Wenn Sie keinen Nachttisch haben oder dieser sehr klein ist, installieren Sie eine tief hängende Deckenlampe nahe am Bett.

Si vous ne disposez pas de table de nuit ou si elle est très petite, vous accrochez une lampe au plafond et vous la faites descendre à proximité du lit.

Heeft u geen nachtkastje of is die heel klein, verlicht dan met een wandlamp die laag vanaf het plafond op een hoogte dichtbij het bed schijnt.

Create a built-in shelf on the wall. To reduce its weight and make the room seem more uncluttered, paint the inside and back of the shelf the same color as the wall.

Bauen Sie eine Ablage in die Wand ein. Um deren Gewicht zu verringern und damit das Zimmer geräumiger wirkt, streichen Sie sie innen und den Hintergrund in derselben Farbe wie die Wand.

On peut construire dans le mur une étagère en maçonnerie. Pour qu'elle paraisse plus légère et pour mieux dégager la pièce, on peut peindre son intérieur et le fond de la même couleur que le mur.

Bevestig een gemetselde plank aan de muur. Om het gewicht te verminderen en de slaapkamer opgeruimder te laten lijken kunt u de binnenkant en achterkant in dezelfde kleur als de muur schilderen.

Place a narrow shelf above the bed to save space and support paintings and ornaments on the headboard.

Bringen Sie ein paar schmale Regale über dem Bett an, um Platz zu gewinnen und Bilder und Ziergegenstände am Kopfende aufzustellen.

Des étagères étroites au-dessus du lit permettent d'optimiser l'espace et d'accueillir des tableaux et des objets de décoration.

Plaats smalle planken boven het bed voor meer ruimte en om schilderijen en versieringen op het hoofdeinde te laten steunen.

Wall-mounted lights by the bed are perfect to save space on the bedside table and provide very specific lighting for reading.

Mit ein paar Wandlampen beim Bett gewinnt man Platz auf dem Nachttisch und gutes Leselicht.

Les appliques murales à côté du lit libèrent les tables de nuit et apportent un éclairage très adapté à la lecture.

Met wandlampen naast het bed krijgt u meer ruimte op het nachttafeltje en een handige leeslamp.

Combine a writing corner or dressing table and an antique style table to give the bedroom personality.

Richten Sie eine Ecke zum Schreiben oder Schminken mit einem Stilmöbel ein, das dem Schlafzimmer eine persönliche Note gibt.

Une table de style ancien faisant office de bureau ou de coiffeuse apporte une touche personnelle à la chambre.

Richt een schrijfhoekje of opmaaktafel in met een antiek soort tafeltje, dat de slaapkamer persoonlijker maakt.

So that the radiator does not get in the way, build
a bespoke unit around it.

Damit der Heizkörper das Aufstellen von Möbeln an der
Wand nicht behindert, konstruieren Sie ein Möbelstück
nach Maß um ihn herum.

Le radiateur ne doit pas empêcher d'installer des
éléments contre le mur. Il peut être intégré dans un
meuble sur mesure.

Laat de radiator geen belemmering zijn om meubels tegen
de muur te zetten. Maak een meubelstuk op maat waar de
radiator wordt ingebouwd.

Increase the storage capacity of the closet with a half height extension that also defines a dressing area.

Erweitern Sie die den Platz im Schrank durch einen Anbau in halber Höhe, der zudem dazu dient, einen Umkleideraum abzugrenzen.

La capacité de rangement de l'armoire peut être augmentée avec un meuble supplémentaire de hauteur moyenne servant aussi à délimiter un espace pour le dressing.

Vergroot de opbergcapaciteit van de kledingkast met een half zo hoog verlengstuk dat bovendien een kleedruimte kan afbakenen.

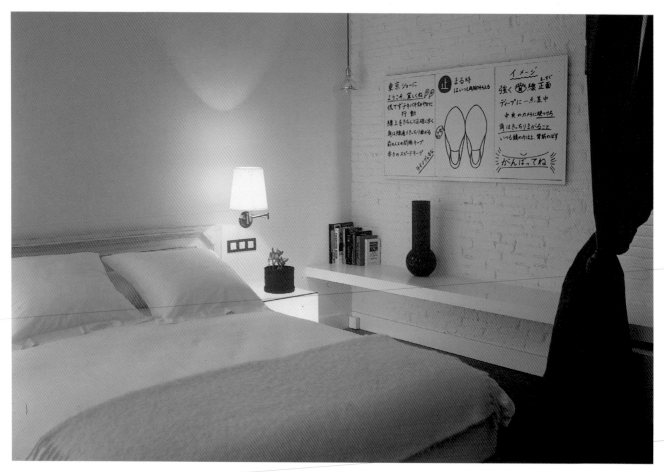

Replace the overhead lighting for several, different points of light to create a cozy atmosphere in the bedroom.

Ersetzen Sie das Deckenlicht durch mehrere verschiedene Lichtquellen, um eine gemütliche Atmosphäre im Schlafzimmer zu schaffen.

L'éclairage zénithal peut être remplacé par différents points de lumière créant une ambiance accueillante dans la chambre.

Vervang verlichting van bovenaf door verschillende lichtpunten om de slaapkamer gezelliger te maken.

Take full advantage of all the walls of the room. Install a shelf on the wall of the headboard and hide it behind the curtains.

Nutzen Sie alle Wände des Zimmers so gut wie möglich aus. Stellen Sie ein Regal an der Wand am Kopfende des Bettes auf, und verstecken Sie es hinter Gardinen.

Vous pouvez exploiter au maximum le potentiel des murs de la pièce : cette bibliothèque installée derrière la tête de lit est cachée par des rideaux.

Benut alle wanden van de slaapkamer maximaal. Installeer een wandmeubel aan de muur van het hoofdeinde van het bed en verberg deze achter een gordijn.

Create a large wardrobe in one corner of the bedroom with a set of shelves behind a semicircular curtain rail.

Konstruieren Sie einen großen Schrank in einer Ecke des Schlafzimmers durch ein Regal, das sich hinter einem Vorhang an einer halbkreisförmigen Schiene befindet.

On peut créer une grande armoire dans un coin de la chambre avec des étagères posées derrière des rideaux accrochés à une tringle en quart de cercle.

Maak een ruime kast in een hoek van de slaapkamer door een wandmeubel achter een gordijn in halfronde rail te zetten.

If you have enough space in the bedroom, erect a partition to separate a small area to use as a dressing room.

Wenn Sie genug Platz im Schlafzimmer haben, errichten Sie eine Zwischenwand, um einen kleinen Bereich abzutrennen und dort den Umkleideraum einzurichten.

Si votre chambre est suffisamment grande, vous pouvez ajouter une cloison délimitant un espace réduit et le transformer en dressing.

Is de slaapkamer ruim genoeg, laat dan een tussenmuur bouwen om een klein gedeelte af te scheiden en een vestiaire in te richten.

Place the dressing room in an area, for example between the bedroom and bathroom, with rails and shelves so that clothes are at hand.

Richten Sie den Umkleideraum in einem Durchgangsbereich, z.B. zwischen Schlafzimmer und Bad ein, mit Kleiderstangen und Regalen, damit die Kleider zur Hand sind.

Le dressing peut se trouver dans une zone de passage, par exemple entre la chambre et la salle de bain, et inclure des étagères pour avoir les vêtements à portée de la main.

Plaats de vestiaire in een looproimte, zoals bijvoorbeeld tussen de slaapkamer en de badkamer, met stangen en planken zodat u kleding bij de hand heeft.

Use boxes to maintain order. It doesn't matter what is visible, especially if it has an attractive design in keeping with the decor of the bedroom.

Greifen Sie zu Schachteln, um Ordnung zu halten. Es macht nichts, dass man sie sieht, vor allem, wenn sie ein attraktives Design haben, das zu der Einrichtung des Schlafzimmers passt.

Les boîtes permettent de ranger correctement les affaires. Elles peuvent être visibles, surtout si elles ont des dessins attrayants en accord avec la décoration de la chambre.

Gebruik dozen om de slaapkamer opgeruimd te houden. Het geeft niet dat ze in het zicht staan, vooral niet als ze een aantrekkelijk design hebben dat overeenstemt met de inrichting van de slaapkamer.

Place a pair of footrests with storage space at the foot of the bed to be able to dress yourself comfortably and have extra space to store blankets.

Stellen Sie zwei Fußstützen, in denen man Dinge aufbewahren kann, am Fußende des Bettes auf, damit Sie sich bequem anziehen können und einen zusätzlichen Platz für die Aufbewahrung der Decken haben.

Vous pouvez poser deux repose-pieds avec coffre de rangement au pied du lit : ils seront utiles au moment de vous habiller et fourniront un espace supplémentaire pour stocker les couvertures.

Plaats enkele bankjes met opbergruimte aan de voet van het bed, zodat u zich comfortabel kunt aankleden en over extra ruimte beschikt om dekens te bewaren.

Incorporate the bathroom into the bedroom through a
built-in bath that can be converted into a bench using
a wooden lid.

Integrieren Sie das Bad ins Schlafzimmer mit einer
eingebauten Badewanne, die sich dank eines Holzdeckels
in eine Bank verwandelt.

La salle de bain peut être intégrée à la chambre : la
baignoire en maçonnerie se transforme en banquette
grâce à une planche en bois.

Integreer de badkamer in de slaapkamer door middel van
een ingemetseld bad dat kan worden omgevormd tot bank
met een houten afdekplaat.

Save space and put part of the bathroom in the bedroom. It is important that the washbowl and vanity unit have the same style as the rest of the bedroom.

Gewinnen Sie Platz, indem Sie einen Teil des Bades im Schlafzimmer installieren. Es ist wichtig, dass das Waschbecken und der Waschtisch im selben Stil wie das übrige Schlafzimmer gehalten sind.

Si on optimise l'espace en intégrant une partie de la salle de bain dans la chambre, le lavabo et son meuble seront du même style que les autres éléments de la pièce.

Verkrijg meer ruimte en plaats een deel van de badkamer in de slaapkamer. Het is belangrijk dat de wastafel en het meubelstuk daaronder dezelfde stijl hebben als die van de rest van de slaapkamer.

Ideally, a faucet attached to the wall is ideal for small washbasins. You can save space and there is no water spray.

Ideal für kleine Waschbecken ist ein Wasserhahn, der direkt aus der Wand kommt. Er spart Platz und verspritzt kein Wasser.

Le robinet sortant directement du mur est la solution idéale pour les petits lavabos. Il gagne de la place et évite les éclaboussures.

Ideaal voor kleine wastafels is een kraan die rechtstreeks uit de muur komt. Hierdoor wordt ruimte bespaard en voorkomt u waterspetters.

Create a harmonious environment in the bedroom using fabrics with the same range of colors and patterns. Smooth textiles are easier to combine.

Schaffen Sie im Schlafzimmer mit Textilien derselben Farb- und Musterskala eine harmonische Atmosphäre. Einfarbige Textilien kann man leichter kombinieren.

Les tissus appartenant à la même gamme de couleurs et d'imprimés créent une atmosphère harmonieuse dans la chambre. Les tissus unis sont plus faciles à associer.

Zorg voor een harmonieuze sfeer in de slaapkamer met textiel in hetzelfde kleurengamma en bedrukte stof. Effen stoffen zijn gemakkelijker te combineren.

Play with the combination of different textures to visually enhance the room, but always use the same range of tones to convey a sense of tranquility.

Spielen Sie mit der Kombination verschiedener Texturen, um das Schlafzimmer optisch interessanter zu machen, aber wählen Sie immer dieselbe Farbskala um einen Eindruck von Ruhe zu vermitteln.

L'association de plusieurs matières enrichit visuellement la chambre, à condition que l'on respecte toujours la même gamme de couleurs pour transmettre une sensation de tranquillité.

Speel met een combinatie van verschillende texturen om de slaapkamer visueel te verrijken, maar altijd binnen hetzelfde kleurengamma, voor een gevoel van rust.

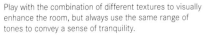

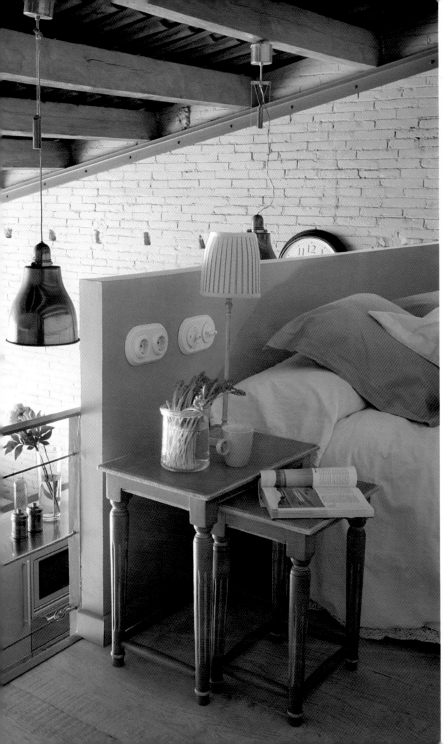

Double-height houses are ideal for a bedroom in the mezzanine. For increased privacy, place a small wall on the side that is connected to the rest of the house.

Die Häuser von doppelter Höhe sind ideal für den Einbau des Schlafzimmers im Halbgeschoss. Für mehr Privatsphäre bringen Sie an der Seite, die es mit der übrigen Wohnung verbindet, eine niedrige Mauer an.

Les maisons sur deux niveaux sont idéales pour installer la chambre à coucher dans la mezzanine. Un muret du côté communicant avec le reste de la maison vous aidera à préserver votre intimité.

Huizen met twee hoogtes zijn ideaal om de slaapkamer op de tussenverdieping in te richten. Plaats voor meer privacy een muurtje aan de kant die in verbinding staat met de rest van de woning.

Use the wall behind the bed as a large headboard, with cladding or painted different than the rest of the walls.

Nutzen Sie die Wand, an der das Bett steht, als ein großformatiges Kopfende mit einer Täfelung oder Farbe, die sich von denen der anderen Wände unterscheidet.

Le mur situé derrière le lit devient une tête de lit de grandes dimensions, à l'aide d'un revêtement ou d'une peinture qui diffère de ceux des autres.

Gebruik de muur waartegen het bed komt te staan als een hoofdeinde met grote afmetingen, met bekleding of een verflaag die anders is dan de overige muren.

Choose special wallpaper, paste it with glue to the wall and border it with a frame in a matching color.

Wählen Sie eine besondere Tapete, leimen Sie sie an die Wand und rahmen Sie sie mit einer Zierleiste in einer passenden Farbe.

Vous pouvez choisir un papier peint spécial, le coller au mur et l'encadrer avec une moulure ayant une couleur qui s'accorde avec celle du papier.

Kies een speciaal behang, plak het tegen de muur en omlijst het met gedecoreerd lijstwerk in een bijpassende kleur.

Bespoke closets make the most of space. Although they are more expensive than standard units, there are many more benefits in terms of storage solutions.

Maßgefertigte Schränke nutzen den Platz am besten aus. Auch wenn sie etwas teurer als die Standardmöbel sind, überwiegen die Vorteile in Bezug auf die Aufbewahrungsmöglichkeiten bei weitem.

Les armoires sur mesure permettent d'exploiter au maximum l'espace disponible. Même si elles sont plus chères que les meubles standard, elles présentent des solutions de rangement beaucoup plus intéressantes.

Met op maat gemaakte kasten maakt u optimaal gebruik van de ruimte. Hoewel ze iets duurder zijn dan standaardmeubelen, zijn de voordelen qua bergruimte veel groter.

If the closets are the same tone as the walls of the bedroom, it will seem visually larger.

Wenn die Schränke im selben Farbton wie die Wände gehalten sind, sieht das Schlafzimmer viel größer aus.

Si les armoires reprennent la couleur des murs, la chambre paraîtra beaucoup plus grande.

Als de kledingkasten dezelfde kleur hebben als de muren van de kamer, lijkt de slaapkamer op het oog ruimer.

Who said the bed had to be stuck to the wall? If you have enough space leave an area around the bed so you can walk around it.

Wer sagt, dass das Bett immer an der Wand stehen muss? Wenn der Raum groß genug ist, lassen Sie Platz frei, um leichter um dieses Möbelstück herumgehen zu können.

Qui a dit que le lit doit être toujours contre le mur ? Si vous avez suffisamment de place, vous pouvez laisser de l'espace autour de ce meuble pour faciliter la circulation.

Wie zegt dat het bed altijd tegen de muur moet staan? Heeft u voldoende ruimte, laat dan loopruimte open rondom het bed.

A bespoke piece of furniture has two uses such as this unit that can be used as a chest of drawers and a bed.

Geben Sie einem einzigen maßgefertigten Möbelstück zwei Verwendungszwecke, wie diesem, das als Schrank oder Kommode und als Bett dient.

Ce meuble sur mesure a une double fonction : celle d'armoire ou commode et de lit.

Gebruik een op maat gemaakt meubelstuk voor twee doeleinden, zoals deze, die dienst doet als kledingkast en als bed.

Build a platform at a distinct height to create a relaxation area and make use of the space for low closet space.

Errichten Sie eine Plattform in einer gewissen Höhe, um dort einen Ruhebereich zu schaffen und die Lücke für niedrige Schränke auszunutzen.

Comment construire une plateforme à une hauteur différente pour créer une zone de repos et profiter de l'espace vide pour installer des armoires basses.

Bouw een platform op een bepaalde hoogte voor een ontspanningsruimte en benut de opening voor lage kasten.

Create a different space with a built-in bed or a mattress placed directly on an oriental style ground level platform.

Schaffen Sie einen besonderen Raum mit einem eingebauten Bett oder legen Sie die Matratze im orientalischen Stil auf ein Podest direkt auf den Boden.

Vous pouvez créer un espace différent avec un lit en maçonnerie ou installer le matelas sur un dénivelé à l'oriental, c'est-à-dire à même le sol.

Creëer een originele ruimte met een gemetselde bad, of leg de matras direct op een verhoging vlak boven de grond, in oosterse stijl.

In a loft, install large format panels to increase privacy in the bedroom.

In einem *loft* installieren Sie großformatige Wandplatten, um dem Schlafzimmer Privatsphäre zu verleihen.

Dans un loft, des panneaux de grandes dimensions préservent l'intimité de la chambre à coucher.

Installeer in een *loft* panelen van groot formaat voor meer privacy in de slaapkamer.

A linear photo arrangement is perfect to decorate a wall behind a bed without a headboard.

Eine Reihe von Fotos in einer Linie aufgehängt, ist perfekt, um die Wand, an der das Bett steht, zu dekorieren, wenn man auf das Kopfteil verzichtet.

Une composition de photos alignées est parfaite pour décorer le mur auquel le lit est adossé et permet de se passer de la tête de lit.

Een compositie van foto's op een rechte lijn is perfect om de muur waartegen het bed staat te versieren en af te zien van een hoofdeinde.

A metal rail and shelf structure, plus a drawer on wheels is enough to create a reasonable closet space.

Eine Metallstruktur mit Stange und Regalbrett und ein Schubladenschrank mit Rädern genügen, um einen Schrank mit beträchtlichem Fassungsvermögen zu schaffen.

Une structure métallique avec étagères, penderie et meuble à tiroirs sur roulettes suffit à créer une grande armoire.

Een metalen structuur met een stang en plank naast een ladenkast op wieltjes is voldoende om een kledingkast met behoorlijke inhoud te creëren.

DINING ROOM
ESSZIMMER
SALLE À MANGER
EETKAMER

Define the dining room space with a bright colored rug, or different flooring.

Grenzen Sie den Essplatz durch einen Teppich in einer auffallenden Farbe oder einen unterschiedlichen Bodenbelag ab.

On peut délimiter l'espace de la salle à manger avec un tapis d'une couleur vive ou un revêtement de sol différent.

Definieer de ruimte van de eetkamer met een vloerkleed in een opvallende kleur of met verschillende vloertegels.

Another way to define the dining area is by choosing furniture in a color that makes the space stand out.

Eine andere Art, den Essplatz abzugrenzen, ist, das Mobiliar in einer Farbe zu wählen, die sich von der Umgebung abhebt.

Une autre manière pour délimiter la salle à manger consiste à choisir des meubles d'une couleur qui se détache des autres.

Een andere manier om de eetkamer af te bakenen is om te kiezen voor meubilair in een kleur die opvalt in de ruimte.

The transparent acrylic or glass tables and chairs visually
lighten the space as they allow light to pass through.

Tische und Stühle aus Glas oder durchsichtigem
Metacrylat wirken leicht, weil sie das Licht durchlassen.

Les tables et les chaises en verre ou en méthacrylate
allègent visuellement l'espace car elles permettent
à la lumière de passer.

Glazen of transparant methacrylaat tafels en stoelen
maken de kamer visueel ruimer omdat zij licht doorlaten.

Chairs do not have to have the same style as the table. Be adventurous with contrasting textures and shapes to create a unique and cozy dining room.

Die Stühle müssen nicht unbedingt denselben Stil wie der Tisch haben. Seien Sie wagemutig mit kontrastierenden Materialien und Formen, um einen so persönlichen wie gemütlichen Essplatz einzurichten.

Les chaises ne doivent pas forcément être dans le même style que la table : vous pouvez oser et créer des contrastes de matériaux et de formes donnant vie à une salle à manger à la fois personnelle et accueillante.

De stoelen hoeven niet persé dezelfde stijl als de tafel te hebben. Durf te spelen met contrasten in texturen en vormen, voor een zowel persoonlijke als gezellige eetkamer.

Adapt furniture to each space and combine benches, stools and chairs around one dining room table while maintaining the same style as far as possible.

Passen Sie die Möbel an jeden Raum an, und kombinieren Sie Bänke, Hocker und Stühle um einen Esstisch, und behalten Sie dabei so weit wie möglich denselben Stil bei.

On peut adapter les meubles à chaque espace et associer des bancs, des tabourets et des chaises autour de la même table, tout en essayant de respecter le même style.

Pas de meubels aan iedere ruimte aan en combineer banken, krukjes en stoelen rond een eettafel en houd daarbij zoveel mogelijk dezelfde stijl aan.

More guests can be seated at a long narrow dining room table than a square table.

An einen langen und schmalen Esstisch passen mehr Tischgenossen als an einen quadratischen Tisch.

Une table de salle à manger longue et étroite peut accueillir plus de convives qu'une table carrée.

Aan een lange, smalle eettafel kunnen meer eters plaatsnemen dan aan een vierkante.

A round table is ideal for saving space when you don't have much of it.

Ein runder Tisch ist ideal, um Platz zu sparen, wenn das Esszimmer klein ist.

Une table ronde est la solution idéale pour gagner de la place lorsque les mètres carrés de la salle à manger manquent.

Een ronde tafel is ideaal om ruimte te creëren in een kleine eetkamer.

Put the table against the wall if the dining room space is very small, and make the area stand out with a large, bright lamp.

Stellen Sie den Tisch an die Wand, wenn es im Essbereich wenig Platz gibt und betonen Sie den Platz mit einer großen Lampe von auffallender Farbe.

Si l'espace est réduit, vous pouvez adosser la table au mur et mettre en évidence une lampe de plafond de grandes dimensions d'une couleur vive.

Is er weinig plaats voor een eethoek, zet de tafel dan tegen de muur aan en laat de ruimte beter tot zijn recht komen door een grote lamp in een opvallende kleur.

Use different colored pairs of chairs from the same range to create a dynamic dining room.

Stellen Sie verschiedenfarbige Stühle eines Sortiments paarweise auf, um den Essplatz dynamisch zu gestalten.

Pour dynamiser la salle à manger, vous pouvez placer les chaises par deux, de couleurs différentes mais dans la même gamme.

Plaats de stoelen twee aan twee, in verschillend kleuren binnen hetzelfde gamma voor meer dynamiek in de eetkamer.

Opt for an extendable table that can be opened out easily so that the dining room can adapt to the number of guests.

Stellen Sie einen Ausziehtisch mit einem einfachen Ausziehmechanismus auf, damit der Essplatz für Essen mit Gästen angepasst werden kann.

Une table à rallonge avec un système d'ouverture simple permet d'adapter la salle à manger aux repas avec des invités.

Installeer een uittrekbare tafel met een eenvoudig uittreksysteem zodat de eetkamer kan worden aangepast als er gasten komen eten.

Instead of a large, strong table that takes up the center of the room, use two small tables that can be joined together for more flexibility.

An Stelle eines großen, massiven Tisches, der das gesamte Zentrum des Essbereiches einnimmt, stellen Sie zwei kleine Tische, die man zusammenstellen kann. Damit gewinnen Sie Flexibilität.

Remplacer une table grande et massive qui remplit la partie centrale de la salle à manger par deux petites tables pouvant s'unir donne une plus grande flexibilité.

Installeer, in plaats van een grote, massieve tafel die de centrale ruimte van de eetkamer in beslag neemt, twee kleine tafels die aan elkaar kunnen worden geschoven, voor meer flexibiliteit.

Opt for designer chairs a different color from the table so that they stand out and define the style of the dining room.

Wählen Sie Stühle in einem vom Tisch unterschiedenen Design und anderer, damit sie die Hauptrolle spielen und den Stil des Essplatzes bestimmen.

Le choix de chaises qui diffèrent de la table par leur dessin et par leur couleur en fait le point de mire de la salle à manger et définit son style.

Kies design stoelen in een andere kleur dan de tafel, zodat ze het middelpunt vormen en bepalend zijn voor de stijl van de eetkamer.

A fireplace is ideal for separating the dining room from the living room because it creates a partial physical barrier but both spaces are still connected.

Ein Kamin ist ideal, um das Ess- vom Wohnzimmer zu trennen, weil er eine teilweise, konkrete Barriere bildet, die die Räume unterteilt und gleichzeitig verbindet.

La cheminée est la solution idéale pour séparer la salle à manger du salon : elle crée une barrière physique partielle permettant aux deux espaces de continuer à communiquer.

Een haard is ideaal om de eetkamer van de zitkamer af te scheiden, omdat het een gedeeltelijke fysieke barrière vormt waardoor beide ruimtes echter nog steeds met elkaar in verbinding staan.

An effective way to separate the dining room from the living room is using a long console table located at the back of the sofa.

Eine wirkungsvolle Art, den Essbereich vom Wohnzimmer zu trennen, bildet eine lange Konsole an der Hinterwand des Sofas.

La salle à manger peut être séparée du salon par une longue console placée contre le dossier du canapé.

Een efficiënte manier om de eetkamer van de zitkamer te scheiden is door middel van een lange console, aan de achterkant van de bank.

Choose natural elements to create a timeless centerpiece that matches all styles.

Entscheiden Sie sich für Elemente aus der Natur, um eine zeitlose Tischdekoration zu gestalten, die zu allen Stilen passt.

On peut emprunter des éléments à la nature pour créer un centre de table atemporel en harmonie avec tous les styles.

Kies elementen die uit de natuur komen om een tijdloze salontafel in te richten, die combineert met alle stijlen.

For an elegant meal with guests, use one or two ranges of colors and materials that blend together.

Für ein elegantes Essen mit Gästen verwenden Sie nur eine oder zwei Farbskalen und Materialien, die zueinander passen.

Pour un repas élégant avec des invités, vous ne choisirez qu'une ou deux gammes de couleurs et des éléments qui vont ensemble.

Gebruik, voor een elegant etentje met gasten, slechts een of twee kleurengamma's en materialen die onderling combineren.

Choose an eye-catching rug to make a dining room
in neutral colors stand out.

Wählen Sie einen Teppich mit auffallenden Motiven, um
einen Essplatz, in dem neutrale Farben vorherrschen,
hervorzuheben.

Un tapis aux motifs voyants rehausse les tons d'une salle
à manger dont la gamme dominante est neutre.

Kies een vloerkleed met in het oog springende motieven
om het accent te leggen op de eetkamer waarin neutrale
kleuren de boventoon voeren.

A classic way to integrate the dining room into the living room is using the same materials for the furniture and in particular the same range of colors.

Eine klassische Art, den Essplatz in das Wohnzimmer zu integrieren ist, dieselben Materialien und vor allem dieselbe Farbskala für das Mobiliar zu verwenden.

Une manière classique pour intégrer la salle à manger au salon consiste à choisir les mêmes matériaux pour le mobilier et tout particulièrement, la même gamme de couleurs.

Een klassieke manier om de eetkamer in de zitkamer te integreren is door gebruik te maken van dezelfde materialen voor het meubilair en met name hetzelfde kleurenkleurengamma.

If the table is long, fit at least two equidistant lamps.

Wenn der Tisch lang ist, sollte man wenigstens zwei Hängelampen im gleichen Abstand installieren.

Si la table est longue, il faut installer au moins deux plafonniers équidistants.

Als de tafel lang is moeten er tenminste twee plafondlampen worden opgehangen, op gelijke afstand van elkaar.

To create a colonial-style dining room choose natural looking wooden table and chairs in white, with natural fiber elements.

Für einen Essplatz im Kolonialstil suchen Sie Tisch und Stühle aus Naturholz oder weiß gestrichen mit Elementen aus Naturfaser aus.

Vous pouvez créer une salle à manger de style colonial avec des chaises et une table en bois naturel ou patinées en blanc, avec des éléments en fibres naturelles.

Zoek, om een eetkamer in koloniale stijl in te richten, stoelen en een tafel van natuurlijk of wit gelakt hout, met elementen van natuurvezel.

A contemporary dining room integrates wood and metal furniture with a sleek design.

Ein Essplatz in modernem Stil besteht aus einer Kombination von Möbeln aus Holz und Metall mit klarem Design.

Una salle à manger de style contemporain mélange des meubles en bois et en métal au dessin épuré.

Een eetkamer in eigentijdse stijl vormt een eenheid door houten en metalen meubels met een verfijnd ontwerp.

BATHROOM
BAD
SALLE DE BAINS
BADKAMER

Built-in bathtubs make better use of space and benches and shelves can be incorporated in the same structure. It is important that the cladding does not filter water.

Eingebaute Badewannen nutzen den Platz besser aus und ermöglichen außerdem Bänke und Regale derselben Struktur anzubauen. Es ist sehr wichtig, darauf zu achten, dass die Beschichtung kein Wasser durchlässt.

Les baignoires en maçonnerie optimisent l'espace, permettant de réunir dans la même structure des surfaces d'appoint et des étagères. Il est très important de choisir un revêtement étanche.

Gemetselde badkuipen benutten de ruimte beter en maken het bovendien mogelijk om banken en planken daarnaast te creëren, alle in dezelfde structuur. Houd er bij de bekleding rekening mee dat het geen water doorlaat.

Fully integrate the bath by cladding it with the same material as the floor and the wall; this will visually enlarge the bath area.

Wenn Sie die Badewanne in derselben Weise wie den Boden und die Wand beschichten, passt alles zusammen, und das Bad wirkt größer.

Revêtir la baignoire avec le même matériau que le sol et le mur permet de l'intégrer complètement à l'ensemble et élargit visuellement la surface de la salle de bain.

Als u de badkuip op dezelfde wijze betegeld als de vloer en de muur, is die steen helemaal geïntegreerd en lijkt het gedeelte van de badkuip groter.

A low wall around the tub fills the angled corners in irregular-shaped baths, and creates surfaces to store shampoo bottles, soap, sponge, etc.

Eine niedrige Ummauerung der Badewanne füllt die Ecken von Badezimmern mit unregelmäßigem Grundriss und schafft Ablageflächen für Shampoo-Flaschen, Seife, Schwamm, usw.

Un muret autour de la baignoire remplit les coins des salles de bain au plan irrégulier et crée des surfaces supplémentaires pour poser le shampoing, le savon, l'éponge, etc.

Een muurtje rond de badkuip vult de hoeken in badkuipen met onregelmatige bouw en creëert oppervlakken om shampooflessen, zeep, sponzen etc. neer te leggen.

Install a shower personal cleanliness and an attached bath to enjoy long relaxing baths: the perfect combination that does not require too much space.

Eine Dusche für die Körperpflege und daneben eine Badewanne, um lange ¨Ruhebäder zu genießen: eine perfekte Kombination, die nicht zu viel Platz verlangt.

Une douche pour se laver et une baignoire pour profiter de longs bains relaxants : une combinaison parfaite qui ne demande pas trop d'espace.

Een douche voor lichaamsverzorging en een badkuip om te genieten van lang badderen: een perfecte combinatie die niet al te veel ruimte inneemt.

Use the wall cladding to differentiate and identify the bathtub area and the shower area.

Verwenden Sie verschiedene Wandverkleidungen, um die Bereiche von Badewanne und Dusche abzugrenzen.

Le revêtement du mur sert à différencier la partie occupée par la baignoire de celle où se trouve la douche.

Gebruik de betegeling van de muur om onderscheid te maken tussen de zone van de badkuip en de douche en deze te definiëren.

Sliding door screens do not require extra space for when the door is open and does not disrupt movement in other areas of the bathroom.

Schiebetüren erfordern keinen Extraplatz wenn die Tür offen ist und behindern den Durchgang zu anderen Bereichen des Badezimmers nicht.

Ouvertes, les portes coulissantes n'exigent pas d'espace supplémentaire et n'interrompent pas la circulation avec les autres parties de la salle de bain.

Schermen van schuifdeuren nemen geen extra ruimte in beslag als de vleugel geopend is en vormen geen belemmering voor de doorgang naar andere zones van de badkamer.

A fixed glass panel is enough to prevent splashing on the floor of the shower area.

Eine feste Glaswand genügt, um Spritzer auf dem Boden des Waschbeckenbereichs zu vermeiden.

Une plaque en verre fixe suffit à éviter les éclaboussures au sol autour des lavabos.

Een vast glazen scherm is voldoende om spatten op de grond bij de wastafels te voorkomen.

Install a shower in a transparent glass booth so as not to disrupt the generous amount of natural light.

Um den großzügigen natürlichen Lichteinfall nicht zu behindern, installieren Sie die Dusche in einer durchsichtigen Glaskabine.

Installer la douche dans une cabine en verre transparent permet à la lumière naturelle d'éclairer cette partie de la pièce.

Om de inval van daglicht niet te onderbreken kunt u de douche in een transparante glazen cabine installeren.

Opt for an open partition complete with a fixed glass
to let light into the bathtub.

Entscheiden Sie sich für eine offene Zwischenwand,
die durch ein fest eingebautes Glas ergänzt wird, um Licht
in die Badewanne zu lassen.

Pour laisser passer la lumière jusqu'à la baignoire, vous
pouvez construire une cloison partiellement ouverte,
complétée d'une plaque de verre fixe.

Kies voor een open tussenschot dat afgemaakt wordt
met een vast glas, zodat er licht tot de badkuip door kan
dringen.

If you want privacy when bathing, organize the shower space within a few low built-in walls.

Wenn Sie beim Baden Unabhängigkeit möchten, richten Sie den Duschbereich innerhalb von niedrigen Mauern ein.

Si vous tenez à votre intimité au moment de vous laver, vous pouvez organiser l'espace de la douche à l'intérieur de murets en maçonnerie.

Wilt u privacy tijdens het baden, richt de ruimte van de douche dan in tussen gemetselde muurtjes.

Choose a preferably smooth and light colored fabric for shower curtains so that they integrate into the environment. Fabrics with patterns and many colors are difficult to combine.

Wählen Sie für die Duschvorhänge einen möglichst glatten, hellen Stoff, damit er sich in die Umgebung einfügt. Textilien mit Mustern und vielen Farben sind schwierig zu kombinieren.

Les rideaux de la douche auront de préférence une couleur claire et unie pour mieux s'intégrer à l'environnement. En effet, il est difficile d'associer les textiles imprimés et très colorés.

Kies voor de douchegordijnen van bij voorkeur een effen stof, in een lichte kleur die in de ruimte integreert. Bedrukte en veelkleurige stoffen zijn lastig te combineren.

Ceramic tiling no only resists moisture and it is long-lasting, but it is also available in a range of colors that can create high-contrasting modern bathrooms.

Keramikbeschichtungen lassen keine Feuchtigkeit durch und verändern sich nicht durch Abnutzung. Zudem bieten sie eine große Farbauswahl und ermöglichen die Gestaltung von modernen, kontrastreichen Bädern.

Le carrelage résiste non seulement à l'humidité et à l'usure mais il offre une gamme de couleurs permettant de créer des salles de bain modernes et très audacieuses.

Keramiek bekledingen zijn bestand tegen vocht en zijn slijtvast. Bovendien bieden zij een kleurengamma waarmee moderne badkamers met groot contrast kunnen worden ontworpen.

When the bathroom has colored surfaces, ensure that the textiles (towels and rugs) are of the same tone, to convey harmony and order.

Wenn die Oberflächen des Bades farbig sind, sorgen Sie dafür, dass die Textilien (Handtücher und Badevorleger) denselben Farbton haben, um Harmonie und Ordnung auszustrahlen.

Si la salle de bain présente des surfaces colorées, les textiles – serviettes et tapis de bain – doivent respecter la même tonalité pour transmettre la sensation d'harmonie et d'ordre.

Als de badkamer voldoende oppervlakken in kleur heeft, zorg er dan voor dat de textiel (handdoeken en matjes) dezelfde kleurschakering heeft, om harmonie en orde uit te stralen.

Modern bathrooms normally have plain walls but you may add mosaic tiles to one wall generally the wall behind the vanity unit.

Moderne Bäder haben glatte Wandbeschichtungen, aber man kann eine Wand - normalerweise die, an dem sich das Waschbecken befindet - mit Mosaikfliesen verkleiden.

Les salles de bain modernes ont des revêtements unis, rehaussés – en général sur le mur du meuble du lavabo – par des dessins réalisés avec du carrelage en mosaïque.

Moderne badkamers hebben vlakke bekledingen, maar een wand (in het algemeen die waar het meubelstuk van de wastafel tegenaan staat) met in mozaïek gemaakte tekeningen is toegestaan.

Achieve a personalized style with vinyl painted wallpaper. There are a very wide variety of designs available and it is very easy to replace.

Erreichen Sie einen persönlichen Stil mit einer Vinyltapete. Sie hat den Vorteil, dass sie in vielen verschiedenen Designs erhältlich ist und man sie sehr einfach austauschen kann.

Vous pouvez personnaliser votre salle de bain en choisissant un revêtement en papier peint vinyle. Vous disposez d'une gamme très vaste de dessins et il est très facile à remplacer.

Verkrijg een persoonlijke stijl met vinyl behang. Het voordeel daarvan is de grote verscheidenheid aan tekeningen en dat het eenvoudig te vervangen is.

Small tiles or ceramic mosaics are ideal for small bathrooms and make them look larger.

Kleine Fliesen oder Mosaikfliesen aus Keramik sind für kleine Badezimmer geeignet, da sie diese größer wirken lassen.

Les petits carreaux ou le carrelage en mosaïque conviennent parfaitement aux petites salles de bain, car ils les font paraître plus grandes.

Kleine tegeltjes of keramiek mozaïeken zijn ideaal voor kleine badkamers, omdat ze die groter doen lijken.

The contrast of polished concrete in wet areas with treated wood in the rest of the bathroom creates a modern and elegant ambience.

Der Kontrast von poliertem Zement in der Nasszone mit dem behandelten Holz im Rest des Badezimmers bewirkt eine moderne und elegante Atmosphäre.

Le contraste entre le béton poli, utilisé dans la partie consacrée à l'eau et le bois traité, présent sur la surface restante, crée une atmosphère moderne et élégante.

Het contrast van gepolijste cement in het watergedeelte met behandeld hout in de rest van de badkamer geeft een moderne en elegante sfeer.

To withstand moisture in the bathroom, choose treated wood that is hard and non-porous with an oil finish that works as a thermal insulator.

Für die Feuchtigkeitsresistenz des Bades wählen Sie besonders hartes, mit Öl behandeltes Holz, das wenig porös ist und als Wärmeisolierung dient.

Pour résister à l'humidité de la salle de bain, le bois choisi doit être traité, particulièrement dur, peu poreux et recouvert d'une couche d'huile qui l'isole thermiquement.

Kies, om weerstand te bieden tegen de vochtigheid in de badkamer, voor behandeld, duurzaam en weinig poreus hout met afwerking in olie, voor een warmte-isolerende werking.

Synthetic parquet flooring has designs that resemble different types of wood. They are easily cleaned and withstand moisture.

Böden aus synthetischem Parkett haben ein Design, das den verschiedenen Holzarten ähnelt, und sie habenden großen Vorteil, dass sie feuchtigkeitsresistent und einfach zu reinigen sind.

Les sols en parquet synthétique ont des dessins imitant différents types de bois. Ils résistent à l'humidité et sont faciles à nettoyer.

Synthetische parketvloeren hebben een ontwerp dat lijkt op verschillende soorten hout en hebben het grote voordeel dat ze beter bestand zijn tegen vocht en gemakkelijk te reinigen zijn.

The new ceramic designs have finishes and patterns identical to stone and are cheaper.

Die neuen Keramik-Designs besitzen ähnliche Oberflächen und Motive wie Naturstein und sind billiger.

Les nouveaux motifs des carrelages ont des finitions imitant la pierre et sont très bon marché.

Moderne ontwerpen van keramiek hebben afwerkingen en motieven die identiek zijn aan steen en die goedkoper zijn.

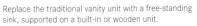

Replace the traditional vanity unit with a free-standing
sink, supported on a built-in or wooden unit.

Ersetzen Sie das traditionelle Waschbecken durch ein
freistehendes Handwaschbecken auf einem eingebauten
Unterschrank oder einem aus Holz.

Le lavabo traditionnel peut être remplacé par un élément
plus original, posé sur un meuble en maçonnerie ou en bois.

Vervang een traditionele wastafel door een los exemplaar
dat op een gemetseld of houten meubelstuk staat

Opt for washbasin proportional to the available area on the vanity unit and leave a space of at least 8 inches on each side so that water does not splash.

Entscheiden Sie sich für ein Waschbecken, das der verfügbaren Fläche der Waschtischplatte proportional ist, und lassen Sie an beiden Seiten mindestens 20 cm Platz übrig, damit das Wasser nicht spritzt.

Le lavabo doit avoir une dimension proportionnelle à la surface disponible du meuble. Il faut laisser au moins 20 cm de chaque côté pour éviter les éclaboussures.

Kies een wastafel waarvan de afmeting proportioneel is met de beschikbare oppervlakte van het werkblad en laat aan weerszijden een ruimte van tenminste 20 cm over, tegen opspattend water.

Take advantage of a built-in unit to create shelves and even a bench to be able to get dressed comfortably.

Nutzen Sie den eingebauten Schrank unter dem Waschbecken, um Regale und sogar eine Bank einzubauen, damit man sich bequem ankleiden kann.

Vous pouvez profiter du meuble en maçonnerie du lavabo pour créer des étagères et une banquette pour vous habiller confortablement.

Benut het gemetselde meubelstuk van de wastafel om planken te maken en zelfs een bankje om u aan te kleden.

The cantilever vanity unit visually lightens this part of the bathroom, in particular when installing two washbasins.

Die freischwebende Waschtischplatte lässt diesen Bereich des Bades leichter wirken, besonders dann, wenn man zwei Waschbecken installiert.

Une étagère murale allège visuellement cette zone de la salle de bain, en particulier si on y installe deux lavabos.

Het vooruitstekende werkblad maakt dit deel van de badkamer optisch lichter, vooral als er twee wastafels worden geïnstalleerd.

Make the most of space with a fitted wardrobe underneath the vanity unit including drawers and open shelves.

Nutzen Sie den Platz mit einem maßgefertigten Schrank unter der Waschtischplatte, der Schubladen und offene Fächer enthält, maximal aus.

Un placard sur mesure sous le lavabo avec des tiroirs et des étagères ouvertes permet d'optimiser l'espace.

Benut de ruimte optimaal met een op maat gemaakte kast onder het werkblad, met daarin laden en open planken.

Install two sturdy wooden shelves: one as a vanity unit to support the washbasin and another as a shelf. Boxes are a great way to keep the objects organized out of sight.

Installieren Sie zwei Regalbretter aus widerstandsfähigem Holz: Eins als Waschtischplatte für die Waschbecken und das andere als Regal. Schachteln sind eine exzellente Lösung, um Gegenstände geordnet außer Sichtweite zu halten.

Vous pouvez installer deux planches en bois résistant servant respectivement de plan d'appui pour le lavabo et d'étagère. Les boîtes sont une excellente solution pour ranger les objets.

Monteer twee resistente houten planken: een die dienst doet als werkblad om de wastafel op te zetten en een als plank. Dozen zijn een uitstekende manier om voorwerpen netjes en buiten het zicht te bewaren.

Place a bench with a shelf underneath the vanity top to store extra towels or a box with items such as the hair dryer, creams, extra toilet paper, etc.

Stellen Sie eine Bank mit einem Regalfach unter die Waschtischplatte des Waschbeckens, um Handtücher oder eine Schachtel mit Gegenständen wie Föhn, Cremes, Toilettenpapierreserve, usw. unterzubringen.

Vous pouvez placer un tabouret avec étagère sous le plan du lavabo pour y ranger les serviettes ou des boîtes contenant des objets tels le sèche-cheveux, les crèmes, la réserve de papier toilette, etc.

Zet een bankje met een plank onder het werkblad van de wastafel, om schone handdoeken op te leggen, of een doos om voorwerpen zoals de föhn, crèmes, of toiletpapier in op te bergen.

The fluid and dynamic forms of the washbasin design makes them striking decorative objects in the bathroom.

Die fließenden und dynamischen Formen der Designer-Waschbecken verwandeln diese in dekorative Objekte, die das Bad zu etwas Besonderem machen.

Les formes fluides et dynamiques des lavabos design en font des objets de décoration qui enrichissent la salle de bain.

Design wastafels met vloeiende en dynamische vormen maken deze tot decoratieve voorwerpen die de badkamer accentueren.

There are many different ways to display the toilet paper beyond the traditional cylinder attached to the wall. Opt for boxes and floor stands that are easier to adapt to the space.

Außer dem traditionellen an der Wand befestigten Rollen gibt es viele Möglichkeiten, das Toilettenpapier anzubringen. Entscheiden Sie sich für Kästen und Ständer, die sich leichter an den Raum anpassen.

Outre le traditionnel cylindre collé au mur, il existe de nombreuses façons de poser le papier toilette : les boîtes et les supports sur pied s'adaptent plus facilement à l'espace.

Naast cilindervormige toiletrolhouders zijn veel andere manieren om het toiletpapier te bewaren. Kies bijvoorbeeld voor dozen en staanders die eenvoudiger kunnen worden aangepast aan de ruimte.

Separating the toilet with a sliding door or stone wall
is practical for homes with one bathroom.

Die Trennung der Sanitärzone durch eine Schiebetür oder
niedrige Mauer ist sehr praktisch für Wohnungen mit nur
einem Bad.

Séparer les sanitaires du reste de la salle de bain par
une porte coulissante ou un mur en maçonnerie est une
solution très pratique.

De afscheiding van het toiletgedeelte door een schuifdeur
of gemetselde muur is heel praktisch voor huizen met
slechts een badkamer.

If the shower and the toilets are installed on the same wall, maximize space with a partition to separate them and a door to give them independence.

Wenn die Dusche und die Toilette an derselben Wand installiert sind, optimieren Sie den Platz mit einer Zwischenwand, um diese Bereiche zu trennen und einer Tür, um sie voneinander unabhängig zu machen.

Si la douche et les sanitaires sont installés sur le même mur, vous pouvez optimiser l'espace avec un muret qui le sépare et une porte qui les rend indépendants.

Als de douche en het toilet tegen een muur zijn geïnstalleerd, optimaliseer de ruimte dan met een tussenschot om deze van elkaar te scheiden en een deur voor onafhankelijke ruimtes.

Convert your bathroom into a spa and place the bathtub at ground level to create breadth.

Sorgen Sie dafür, dass Ihr Bad einem *spa* ähnelt und lassen Sie die Badewanne in den Boden ein, um Geräumigkeit zu gewinnen.

Votre salle de bain peut avoir l'allure d'un spa : la baignoire à même le sol permet de gagner de l'espace.

Geef uw badkamer het uiterlijk van een *spa* en laat de badkuip in de vloer leggen om ruimte te besparen.

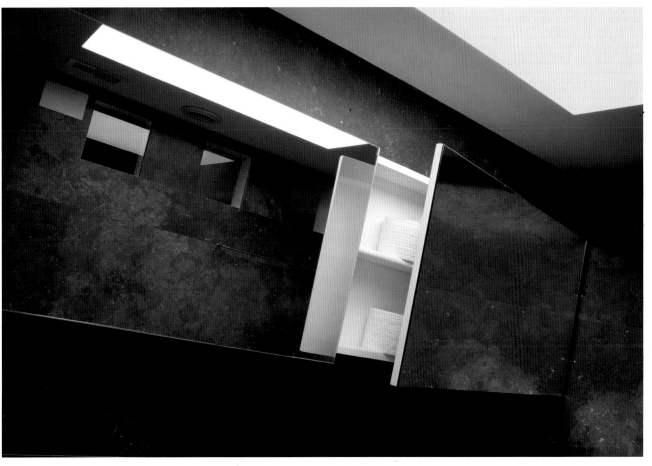

The dark toned cladding gives a contemporary but makes the bathroom look smaller. However, a generous amount of natural light offsets and extends the space visually.

Die Beschichtung mit dunklen Farbtönen verleiht dem Bad einen modernen Anstrich, lässt es aber kleiner wirken. Durch einen großzügigen Lichteinfall wird dies jedoch ausgeglichen und der Raum sieht größer aus.

Le revêtement sombre donne un air contemporain à la salle de bain mais la rend plus petite. Une grande ouverture peut compenser, apportant de la lumière et augmentant visuellement l'espace.

Bekleding in donkere kleuren zorgen voor een eigentijdse look, maar doen de badkamer kleiner lijken. Als er veel daglicht naar binnen schijnt wordt dit gecompenseerd en lijkt de ruimte optisch groter.

Leave a blank strip above the tiles so that the wall seems higher.

Lassen Sie einen weißen Streifen über der gefliesten Fläche frei, damit die Wand höher wirkt.

Le mur paraît plus haut si on laisse une bande blanche au-dessus du carrelage.

Laat boven de zone met tegeltjes een strook wit open, zodat de muur hoger lijkt.

Use the bathroom to store accessories such as hats and pendants, and convert this space into a dressing room.

Nutzen Sie das Bad, um Accessoires wie Hüte und Anhänger aufzubewahren und gewinnen Sie wieder die Funktion dieses Raumes als Boudoir.

Vous pouvez utiliser la salle de bain pour ranger des accessoires tels les chapeaux et les pendentifs, comme sur une coiffeuse.

Gebruik de badkamer om accessoires zoals hoeden en hangers te bewaren, en herstel in deze ruimte het concept van toilettafel in ere.

To create a warm ambience, decorate with paintings and photo frames of materials and colors in the same range as the mirror.

Um eine warme Atmosphäre zu schaffen, dekorieren Sie den Spiegel mit Bildern und Fotorahmen aus Materialien und Farben im gleichen Stil.

Pour créer une atmosphère chaude, vous pouvez décorer la pièce avec des tableaux et des porte-photos conçus dans des matériaux et des couleurs de la même gamme que le miroir.

Voor een warme sfeer kunt u decoreren met schilderijen en fotolijsten van materialen en kleuren in hetzelfde gamma als de spiegel.

Why not place a table lamp in the bathroom? You will give the space its own personality with this object that is not normally seen in the bathroom.

Überraschen Sie mit einer Tischlampe im Bad. Durch dieses weniger traditionelle Stilmittel verleihen Sie diesem Raum Persönlichkeit.

Une lampe de table dans la salle de bain crée un effet de surprise. Ce choix moins traditionnel vous permettra de personnaliser cet espace.

Creëer een verrassend effect met een tafellamp in de badkamer. Met dit minder traditionele hulpmiddel geeft u persoonlijkheid aan deze ruimte.

An easy way to counteract the coldness of this microcement finish is to display decorative details in warm materials such as natural fiber and wood.

Eine einfache Art, der Kälte, die die Mikrozement-Flächen ausstrahlen entgegenzuwirken besteht darin, dekorative Objekte aus warmen Materialien wie Naturfaser und Holz aufzustellen.

Une manière facile pour mitiger la froideur transmise par le revêtement en microciment consiste à ajouter des détails décoratifs conçus avec des matériaux chauds comme la fibre naturelle et le bois.

Een eenvoudige manier om de koude sfeer die de afwerking in microcement uitademt te neutraliseren is om decoratieve details van warme materialen zoals natuurvezel en hout neer te zetten.

Towels in one color add to the elegance of the bathroom. Try and use the same color for the rest of textiles, such as the mat or shower curtain.

Einfarbige Handtücher tragen dazu bei, das Bad eleganter zu machen. Umso mehr, wenn die anderen Textilien wie die Fußmatte oder der Duschvorhang vom selben Farbton sind.

Les serviettes d'une couleur unies rendent la salle de bain plus élégante. Si le reste des textiles – le tapis de bain ou les rideaux de la douche - sont dans la même tonalité, l'effet est renforcé.

Handdoeken in dezelfde kleur geven de badkamer iets elegants. Het is nog beter als ook de rest van de textiel, zoals het matje of het douchegordijn dezelfde tint hebben.

Make small bathrooms stand out with small decorative details that do not take up space such as a panel to support and frame the mirror.

Werten Sie sehr kleine Bäder mit dekorativen Details auf, die keinen Platz wegnehmen, wie ein Paneel, das den Spiegel hält und einrahmt.

Vous pouvez enrichir les salles de bain très petites avec des détails de décoration qui ne prennent pas de place, comme un panneau servant à suspendre et encadrer le miroir.

Gebruik in hele kleine badkamers decoratieve details die niet veel ruimte innemen, zoals een paneel dat dienst doet om de spiegel te ondersteunen en in te lijsten.

If you opt for wooden furniture, the mirror frame should be in the same material and color to create a harmonious ensemble.

Wenn der Waschtisch des Waschbeckens aus Holz ist, sollte der Rahmen des Spiegels aus demselben Material sein, um ein harmonisches Ensemble zu schaffen.

Si le meuble du lavabo est en bois, il vaut mieux que le cadre du miroir soit dans le même matériau et couleur pour créer un ensemble harmonieux.

Is het meubelstuk van de wastafel van hout, laat de omlijsting van de spiegel dan van hetzelfde materiaal zijn en dezelfde kleur hebben, om een harmonieus geheel te krijgen.

Mirrors with shallow depth wall cabinets offer a quick overview of all articles, which are easier to find without knocking over the other articles.

Spiegel mit Wandschränken, die nicht zu tief sind, bieten einen schnelleren Überblick über alle Artikel, so dass man sie leichter greifen kann, ohne andere umzuwerfen.

Les miroirs avec des placards peu profonds offrent une vue générale plus rapide de tous les articles, plus faciles à attraper sans déplacer les autres.

Spiegels met ondiepe wandkasten bieden een sneller overzicht van alle artikelen, die eenvoudig kunnen worden gepakt zonder de andere om te gooien.

OUTDOORS

IM FREIEN

L'EXTÉRIEUR

IN DE BUITENLUCHT

Use cushions and garden beds to create a relaxation area. They are very easy to transport and store.

Verwenden Sie mit Kissen und Gartenliegen, um eine Ruhezone zu gestalten. Sie sind sehr leicht zu transportieren und aufzubewahren.

Coussins, transats et lits de jardin créent une zone de relaxation. Ils sont très faciles à transporter et à ranger.

Neem uw toevlucht tot kussens en ligstoelen om een relaxzone te verkrijgen. Ze zijn eenvoudig te verplaatsen en op te bergen.

Hanging hammocks are ideal for relaxation for adults and for children to play with. If you do not have trees to tie them to use a column or fix a hook to the wall.

Hängematten sind ideal zum Ausruhen für Erwachsene und zum Spielen für die Kinder. Wenn Sie keine Bäume haben, um sie daran zu befestigen, benutzen Sie eine Säule oder schlagen Sie einen Haken in die Wand.

Les hamacs suspendus sont une excellente solution pour le repos des adultes et les jeux des enfants. Si vous n'avez pas d'arbres pour les accrocher, vous pouvez utiliser une colonne ou fixer un crochet au mur.

Hangmatten zijn ideaal voor volwassenen om te relaxen en voor kinderen om te spelen. Heeft u geen bomen om deze op te hangen, gebruik dan een zuil of hang ze aan een haak in de muur.

Straw is a good option for the porch roof because it lets air flow freely. Today there are products that help you to maintain it for much longer without it deteriorating.

Stroh ist eine gute Option für das Dach der Veranda, weil es luftdurchlässig ist. Außerdem gibt es heutzutage Produkte, die dazu beitragen, dass es sich viel länger hält, ohne schadhaft zu werden.

Le toit en paille est une bonne option car il laisse circuler l'air. En plus, aujourd'hui il existe des produits qui retardent sa détérioration.

Riet is een goede optie voor het dak van de veranda, omdat dat materiaal lucht doorlaat. Bovendien bestaan er vandaag de dag producten die eraan bijdragen dat ze veel langer meegaan.

Incorporate the living room into the garden through sliding doors blurring the boundaries of the living room, and use the same flooring on the interior and exterior.

Verbinden Sie das Wohnzimmer mit dem Garten durch denselben Bodenbelag draußen wie drinnen und durch Schiebetüren, die, wenn sie geöffnet sind, die Grenzen des Zimmers verwischen.

Les portes coulissantes permettent d'intégrer le salon au jardin : ouvertes, elles effacent les limites de la pièce, grâce aussi au choix du même revêtement de sol à l'intérieur et à l'extérieur.

Integreer de zitkamer met de tuin door middel van schuifdeuren die, als ze worden geopend, de grenzen v an de kamer vervagen en door buiten en binnen dezelfde vloertegels te gebruiken.

Select outdoor furniture made from synthetic fibers that look like interior furniture to create comfy spaces on the porch.

Wählen Sie Außenmöbel aus synthetischen Fasern, die wie Innenmöbel aussehen, um einen gemütlichen Raum auf der Veranda zu schaffen.

Le choix de meubles d'extérieur en fibres synthétiques ressemblant à des éléments d'intérieur crée sous le porche des espaces accueillants.

Kies voor buitenmeubels van synthetische vezels die voor binnen lijken voor gezellige ruimtes onder de overkapping.

Make the most of the porch and recreate a dining area and an outdoor lounge, each well defined by the furniture.

Nutzen sie die Veranda voll aus und gestalten Sie ein Esszimmer und ein Wohnzimmer im Freien, jedes durch das Mobiliar klar definiert.

La création d'une salle à manger et d'un salon en plein air, bien délimités par leur mobilier, permet de profiter au maximum du porche.

Haal het maximale uit de veranda en maak een eetkamer en een zitkamer in de buitenlucht, beide goed afgebakend door middel van het meubilair.

Wood is one of the materials best suited to all styles of outdoor furniture in particular when they are located under a porch protected from the rain.

Holz ist eins der Materialien, das sich am besten an alle Stilarten im Freien anpasst, vor allem, wenn sich die Möbel unter einem Verandadach befinden, das sie vor Regen schützt.

Le bois est l'un des matériaux qui s'adaptent le mieux à tous les styles d'extérieurs, surtout lorsque les meubles sont sous un porche qui les protège de la pluie.

Hout is een van de materialen die zich het beste aanpassen aan alle stijlen voor buiten, met name als de meubels onder een overkapping worden gezet waar ze beschermd zijn tegen de regen.

Add a touch of green to the balcony with a continuous row of shrubs planted in a planter of the same material as the flooring.

Begrünen Sie den Balkon mit einer ununterbrochenen Reihe von Büschen in einem Blumenkasten aus demselben Material, aus dem der Boden besteht.

Vous pouvez ajouter une touche verte à votre balcon avec une rangée ininterrompue d'arbustes plantés dans un bac fait dans le même matériau que le sol.

Geef het balkon een groen accent met een ononderbroken rij struiken in een plantenbak van hetzelfde materiaal als de vloer.

Tall, minimalist, modern pots are ideal for small balconies, as the plants are the focus of attention due to their height. Leave them near the window to bring a touch of green to the interior.

Die modernen, hohen, minimalistischen Blumentöpfe sind ideal für kleine Balkone, da die Pflanzen durch ihre Höhe die Szene beherrschen. Stellen Sie sie in Fensternähe auf, damit sie Grün ins Innere bringen.

Les pots modernes, hauts et minimalistes, sont parfaits pour les petits balcons, car les plantes s'imposent par leur hauteur. Vous pouvez les laisser près de la fenêtre pour qu'ils transmettent une note verte à l'intérieur.

Moderne bloembakken, hoog en minimalistisch, zijn ideaal voor kleine balkons, aangezien de aandacht wordt getrokken door de planten vanwege hun hoogte. Zet ze dicht bij het raam zodat ze het groen naar binnen brengen.

Use plants and shrubs that reach a height of about three feet to define the garden space, thus maintaining privacy without losing the overview.

Verwenden Sie Pflanzen und Büsche, die ungefähr einen Meter hoch werden, um den Garten zu begrenzen. So erhalten Sie die Privatsphäre ohne die Aussicht zu verlieren.

Utiliser des plantes et des arbustes atteignant environ un mètre de hauteur pour délimiter l'espace du jardin permet de préserver son intimité sans renoncer à la vue générale.

Gebruik planten en struiken die ongeveer een meter hoog worden om de tuin af te bakenen, zodat uw privacy behouden blijft zonder dat het uitzicht belemmerd wordt.

To create a small outdoor dining area you only need
a table and two chairs. If they are lightweight, you can
change their position whenever you want.

Um ein kleines Esszimmer im Freien zu schaffen, sind
nur ein Tisch und zwei Stühle nötig. Sie sind leicht zu
transportieren und man kann sie an verschiedenen Orten
des Gartens aufstellen.

Pour créer une petite salle à manger et plein air, il suffit
d'une table et de quelques chaises. Si elles sont faciles à
transporter, vous pouvez changer leur emplacement dans
le jardin.

Voor een kleine eethoek buiten heeft u alleen maar
een tafel en een paar stoelen nodig. Als ze gemakkelijk
verplaatsbaar zijn kunnen ze binnen de tuin worden
verplaatst tegen een andere achtergrond.

Take advantage of large trees to place a dining area under their crown. It's the best way to shelter from the sun.

Nutzen Sie die großen Bäume des Hauses aus, um einen Essplatz unter ihrer Krone einzurichten. Dies ist die beste Art, sich vor der Sonne zu schützen.

Vous pouvez installer une salle à manger sous les grands arbres du jardin. C'est la meilleure façon pour se protéger du soleil.

Gebruik grote bomen in de tuin om er een eethoek neer te zetten. Dat is de beste manier om uit de zon te zitten.

A pine floor is ideal for around the pool as it is very easy to maintain.

Ein Boden aus Pinienholz ist ideal für die Umrandung des Schwimmbeckens, weil er so leicht zu warten ist.

Le plancher en pin, très facile à entretenir, est le revêtement idéal pour le sol autour de la piscine.

Een grenenhouten vloer is ideaal voor rondom het zwembad, vanwege het eenvoudige onderhoud.

Erect a parasol with the mast to one side to make full use of the shadow it creates.

Stellen Sie einen Sonnenschirm mit seitlichem Mast, um den Schatten, den er erzeugt, voll auszunutzen.

Il vaut mieux choisir un parasol ayant un pied décentré pour profiter de toute l'ombre qu'il génère.

Installeer een parasol met een staander aan een kant om van alle schaduw gebruik te kunnen maken.

Light the interior of the pool to prevent accidents at night, it means that it can be used at any time and emphasizes the design.

Beleuchten Sie das Schwimmbecken von innen, um Unfälle in der Nacht zu vermeiden. Die Innenbeleuchtung ermöglicht zudem die Benutzung des Beckens zu jeder Zeit und hebt sein Design hervor.

Éclairer l'intérieur de la piscine permet d'éviter les incidents nocturnes, de l'utiliser à n'importe quel moment de la journée et de mettre en valeur sa forme.

Verlicht het zwembad van binnen om 's avonds ongelukken te voorkomen. Zo kan het zwembad op ieder willekeurig tijdstip gebruikt worden en komt het ontwerp beter tot zijn recht.

The furniture and facilities around the pool should be consistent in the shapes and materials to integrate the entire environment.

Die Möbel und Installationen rund um das Schwimmbecken sollten in Form und Material einheitlich sein, damit alles zu der Umgebung passt

Les meubles et les installations autour de la piscine doivent respecter la cohérence des formes et des matériaux pour s'harmoniser avec l'environnement.

Meubels en voorzieningen rond het zwembad moeten qua vorm en materiaal overeenkomen, zodat de ruimte een eenheid vormt.

Anthracite and aluminum are the main materials used for new outdoor dining table sets, resistant to all kinds of weather.

Aluminium und Anthrazitstoffe, die gegen alle Unbilden des Wetters resistent sind, spielen die Hauptrolle bei den neuen Esszimmermöbeln für draußen.

L'aluminium et le tissu en anthracite sont les stars du nouveau mobilier pour salle à manger d'extérieur, résistant à toutes les intempéries.

Aluminium en antraciet materialen zijn toonaangevend voor de nieuwe tuinmeubelensets en zijn bestand tegen allerlei weersomstandigheden.

Furnish the exterior as if it were interior. Opt for highly durable materials and do not skimp on details such as decorative candles, textiles, carpets and curtains.

Statten Sie die Außenbereiche wie das Innere des Hauses aus, Verwenden Sie widerstandsfähige Materialien und sparen Sie nicht an dekorativen Einzelheiten wie Kerzen, Textilien, Teppichen und Vorhängen.

La décoration extérieure exige la même attention que l'intérieur. Il faut choisir des matériaux très résistants et ne pas lésiner sur les accessoires décoratifs comme les bougies, les tapis et les rideaux.

Richt de buitenruimte net zo in als een interieur. Kies voor degelijke materialen en beknibbel niet op decoratieve details zoals kaarsen, textiel, kleden en gordijnen.

The blinds of a semi-translucent fabric around the porch control the heat and air currents. Raw or very clear colors are best so as not to create a sense of closure.

Die Stores aus einem halbtransparenten Stoff um die Veranda herum regulieren Wärme und Luftzug. Es ist besser, wenn sie naturfarben oder sehr hell sind, damit sie kein Gefühl von Eingeschlossensein erwecken.

Réalisés dans un textile semi-translucide, les stores entourant le porche règlent l'entrée de la chaleur et les courants d'air. Les couleurs claires et l'écru sont à préférer car ils ne provoquent pas la sensation d'enfermement.

Door rolgordijnen van een halfdoorschijnende stof rond de veranda op te hangen, kunnen de warmte en luchtstromen worden gecontroleerd. Deze hebben bij voorkeur naturel of hele lichte kleuren, zodat ze niet het gevoel geven ingesloten te zijn.

Place two wooden veneer panels on the sides of the porch to create a partial enclosure, and paper them with original designs, maintaining the same range of tones as the furniture.

Bringen Sie zwei Paneele aus Furnierholz an den Seiten der Veranda an, um sie teilweise abzuschließen, und tapezieren Sie sie mit originellen Motiven im selben Farbton wie die Möbel.

Deux panneaux en contreplaqué posés sur les côtés du porche ferment partiellement l'espace. Vous pouvez les tapisser de motifs originaux rappelant la même gamme de couleurs que les meubles.

Plaats twee panelen van fineerhout aan weerszijden van de veranda voor een gedeeltelijke afsluiting en hang deze vol met originele motieven, waarbij altijd hetzelfde kleurengamma als van de meubels wordt aangehouden.

Candles create a special atmosphere outdoors. Place them alone or lanterns, on steps, on the edge of the balcony or in the corners of the courtyard.

Kerzen schaffen im Freien eine besondere Atmosphäre. Stellen Sie sie alleine oder innerhalb von Laternen auf, auf Treppenstufen, am Rand des Balkons oder in den Ecken des Patios.

À l'extérieur, les bougies créent une atmosphère spéciale, que vous les placiez toute seules ou dans une lanterne, sur les marches des escaliers, sur la bordure du balcon ou aux coins de la cour.

Kaarsen brengen een speciale sfeer buiten. Plaats ze los of in lantaarns op de treden van de trap, aan de rand van het balkon of in de hoeken van de patio.

Recreates a romantic and functional ambience with wrought iron antique beds that can be used as seats or berths to enjoy long naps outdoors.

Gestalten Sie eine romantische und funktionale Umgebung mit alten schmiedeeisernen Betten, die als Sitzmöbel oder Liegen für lange Siestas im Freien dienen.

On peut recréer une atmosphère romantique et fonctionnelle avec des lits anciens en fer forgé faisant office de siège ou de transat pour profiter de longues siestes en plein air.

Schep een romantische en functionele sfeer met enkel oude smeedijzeren bedden die dienst doen als zitplaatsen of ligstoelen, om te genieten van lange siësta's in de buitenlucht.

Lay rugs outdoors to define ambiences and add warmth and personality to the space.

Legen Sie draußen Teppiche aus, um Bereiche abzugrenzen und der Umgebung Wärme und Persönlichkeit zu verleihen.

Sortir les tapis à l'extérieur aide à créer une atmosphère, apporte de la chaleur et personnalise l'espace.

Haal de vloerkleden naar buiten om ruimtes af te bakenen en voor een warme en persoonlijke sfeer.

The creation of exterior points of light is as important as inside the house. Use large lanterns, strings of lights and small spotlights to create a special atmosphere.

Die Installation von Lichtquellen ist draußen genauso wichtig wie im Inneren des Hauses. Verwenden Sie große Laternen, Lichterketten und kleine Scheinwerfer, um eine besondere Atmosphäre zu schaffen.

L'éclairage est aussi important à l'intérieur qu'à l'extérieur. Grandes lanternes, guirlandes lumineuses et petits lampadaires créent une belle atmosphère.

De creatie van lichtpunten is buiten net zo belangrijk als binnenshuis. Kies voor lantaarns, guirlandes en kleine spots om een speciale sfeer te creëren.

Make use of the slope in the yard to create chill out spaces with cushions on the steps.

Profitieren Sie von den Höhenunterschieden im Patio, um mit Kissen auf den Treppenstufen einen *chill out* Bereich zu schaffen.

Vous pouvez utiliser le dénivelé de la cour pour créer un espace de détente avec des coussins sur les marches.

Benut hoogteverschillen in de patio voor een *chill out* ruimte met kussens op de traptreden.

Les hamacs suspendus sont une excellente solution pour le repos des adultes et les jeux des enfants. Si vous n'avez pas d'arbres pour les accrocher, vous pouvez utiliser une colonne ou fixer un crochet au mur.

TEXTURE AND COLOR

TEXTUR UND FARBE

MATIÈRES ET COULEURS

TEXTUUR EN KLEUR

Les portes coulissantes permettent d'intégrer le salon au jardin : ouvertes, elles effacent les limites de la pièce, grâce aussi au choix du même revêtement de sol à l'intérieur et à l'extérieur.

Le bois est l'un des matériaux qui s'adaptent le mieux à tous les styles d'extérieurs, surtout lorsque les meubles sont sous un porche qui les protège de la pluie.

Yellows, browns and mustard are stimulating and create a feeling of warmth. Use them if you live in a cold area or the room does not receive much sunlight.

Gelb, Ocker und Senf sind anregend und schaffen eine warme Atmosphäre. Verwenden Sie sie, wenn sie in einem kalten Gebiet wohnen, oder das Zimmer nicht viel Sonnenlicht empfängt.

Les couleurs jaune, ocre et moutarde sont stimulantes et génèrent une sensation de chaleur. Elles sont particulièrement adaptées aux régions froides ou aux pièces assez sombres.

Gele, oker en mosterdtinten zijn stimulerend en geven een gevoel van warmte. Gebruik ze als u in een koud gebied woont of als de kamer niet veel zonlicht krijgt.

Apply a different color to one of the surfaces that forms part of the same ambience to highlight structural objects or simply to liven up the room.

Gestalten Sie eine der Flächen, die zur selben Umgebung gehören in einer anderen Farbe, um strukturelle Objekte hervorzuheben oder einfach um den Raum lebendiger wirken zu lassen.

Appliquer une couleur différente à l'une des surfaces d'un même environnement fait ressortir les éléments structuraux ou tout simplement donne plus de vie à l'espace.

Breng een verschillende kleur aan op een van de oppervlaktes die deel uitmaken van dezelfde ruimte om structurele voorwerpen te laten opvallen of om simpelweg meer levendigheid aan het vertrek te geven.

Cold colors such as green are ideal to "cool down" a
south-facing room or a room that is too warm or small.

Kalte Farben, wie Grün, sind ideal um ein Zimmer,
das nach Süden liegt, oder zu warm und klein ist,
«abzukühlen».

Les couleurs froides comme le vert sont idéales pour
« refroidir » une pièce orientée plein sud ou trop chaude
et de dimensions réduites.

Koude kleuren zoals groen zijn ideaal om een kamer op
het zuiden of een te warme en kleine kamer «af te koelen».

For a high ceiling to seem lower it should be painted the same color as the walls.

Damit eine hohe Decke niedriger wirkt, sollte man sie in derselben Farbe wie die Wände streichen.

Pour abaisser visuellement un plafond très haut, il faut le peindre de la même couleur que les murs.

Verf een hoog plafond, om het lager te laten lijken, in dezelfde kleur als de muren.

Color can establish a focal point or create interest in a point of the room, whether it is through painting a wall a different color or through elements such as curtains or rugs.

Die Farbe kann einen Blickpunkt bieten oder das Interesse auf eine Stelle des Zimmers lenken, entweder durch eine Wand in einer anderen Farbe oder durch Elemente wie Vorhänge oder Teppiche.

La couleur permet d'attirer l'attention sur un endroit précis de la maison, par exemple un mur peint d'une couleur différente ou des éléments comme les rideaux ou les tapis.

Kleur kan de aandacht vestigen op een bepaald punt in de kamer. Dat effect kan zowel bereikt worden door een muur in een andere kleur te verven als door middel van elementen zoals gordijnen of vloerkleden.

Using two different colors for walls can achieve interesting results: generating amplitude, visually reducing a space or highlighting a corner.

Wenn man zwei Farben für verschiedene Wände benutzt, kann man interessante Ergebnisse erzielen: Weite schaffen, einen Raum kleiner wirken lassen oder eine Ecke hervorheben.

Peindre deux murs avec deux couleurs différentes permet d'obtenir des résultats intéressants : élargir visuellement l'espace, le réduire ou faire ressortir un angle.

Het gebruik van twee kleuren voor verschillende wanden kan interessante resultaten opleveren: meer ruimte, om een ruimte kleiner te laten lijken of om de aandacht te vestigen op een bepaald hoekje.

Architectural features such as moldings are accentuated when painted a darker or lighter color than the walls.

Architektonische Besonderheiten wie Zierleisten werden hervorgehoben, wenn man sie in einer dunkleren oder helleren Farbe als die Wände streicht.

Les éléments architecturaux, telles les moulures, ressortent du cadre en les peignant avec une couleur plus sombre ou plus claire que le mur.

Bouwkundige kenmerken zoals lijstwerken worden geaccentueerd als ze in een donkerdere of juist lichtere kleur dan de muren worden geschilderd.

If you go for a dark color for the wall, make sure the room is well-lit. If not, it will seem cold and small.

Wenn Sie sich für eine dunkle Wandfarbe entscheiden, sorgen Sie dafür, dass das Zimmer gut beleuchtet ist. Wenn nicht, wirkt es ungemütlich und wirkt kleiner.

Vous pouvez peindre un mur avec une couleur sombre si la pièce est bien éclairée, sinon elle paraîtra très peu accueillante et semblera plus petite.

Kiest u voor een donkere kleur op de muur, doe dat dan in een goed verlichte kamer, anders lijkt hij ongezellig en klein.

Microcement is suitable for all types of surfaces and can be applied over any covering. It is available in a wide range of colors, it does not require sealing and is easily cleaned.

Mikrozement ist für alle Arten von Oberflächen geeignet und kann auf jeden Verputz aufgetragen werden. Es gibt ihn in vielen verschiedenen Farben, er erfordert keine Fugen und ist leicht zu reinigen.

Le microciment est adapté à tout type de surface et peut être posé sur n'importe quel revêtement. Il présente une vaste gamme de couleurs, n'a pas de jointures et est très facile à nettoyer.

Microcement is geschikt voor alle soorten oppervlakken en kan op ieder willekeurige bekleding worden toegepast. Er is een breed kleurengamma voorhanden, er zijn geen voegnaden nodig en het is eenvoudig schoon te maken.

Traditionally used on roofs, slate is now being used on walls even on the interior due to its elegance and easy maintenance.

Traditionell oft für Dächer gebraucht, wird Schiefer dank seiner Eleganz und einfachen Wartung auch für Wände, sogar in Innenräumen gebraucht.

Traditionnellement très employée pour réaliser des toitures, l'ardoise est utilisée aujourd'hui aussi sur les murs intérieurs, car elle est élégante et facile à entretenir.

Leisteen wordt van oudsher veel gebruikt op daken, maar het gebruik daarvan heeft zich uitgebreid tot muren en zelfs binnenshuis dankzij de elegantie en doordat het onderhoudsvriendelijk is.

Stone cladding is no longer synonymous with rustic style. The application of the latest technology gives the porcelain interesting natural stone effects and resistance.

Steinbeschichtung ist nicht mehr gleichbedeutend mit rustikalem Stil. Die Verwendung neuester Technologien verleiht Feinsteingut interessante Natursteineffekte und große Widerstandskraft.

Utiliser la pierre pour revêtir une surface n'est plus synonyme de style rustique. Les dernières technologies confèrent au grès porcelainé des effets intéressants, rappelant la pierre naturelle, et une grande résistance.

Bekleden met steen is niet meer synoniem met een landelijke stijl. De toepassing van de laatste technologieën zorgt ervoor dat aardewerk interessante effecten van natuursteen kan geven en zeer duurzaam is.

Marble is both an elegance and timeless finish. In the kitchen, achieve a striking aesthetic effect by covering the walls and worktops with the same type of marble.

Marmor sieht sehr elegant aus und kommt nie aus der Mode. Erreichen Sie in der Küche einen ästhetischen Eindruck, indem Sie die Wände und die Arbeitsflächen mit derselben Marmorart verkleiden.

Le marbre apporte une touche très élégante et est toujours à la mode. L'utilisation du même type de marbre sur les murs et les plans de travail de la cuisine permet d'obtenir un effet esthétique saisissant.

Marmer geeft een zeer elegante afwerking en raakt nooit uit de mode. In de keuken bereikt u een indrukwekkend esthetisch effect door de muren en werkbladen met hetzelfde type marmer te bekleden.

When deciding on the colors for the walls and furniture, take into account the flooring. Brown-toned flooring will not go well with certain colors for walls and ceilings.

Berücksichtigen Sie den Boden, wenn Sie die Farbe der Wände und der Möbel wählen. Ein Boden in Brauntönen passt nicht allzugut zu mehrfarbigen Wänden und Decken.

Dans le choix de la couleur des murs et des meubles, on doit tenir compte du sol. Un revêtement dans les tons bruns ne s'accordera pas trop aux murs et à un plafond aux couleurs multiples.

Let bij de keuze van de kleur voor muren en meubels op de vloer. Een vloer in bruine tinten doet het niet goed bij muren en plafonds in diverse kleuren.

To get a sense of continuity between the kitchen and the dining room, choose a single light-colored flooring for both environments. Oak is the hardest and most hard-wearing wood.

Um ein Gefühl von Einheitlichkeit von offener Küche und Esszimmer zu erreichen, wählen Sie für beide Bereiche einen einzigen Bodenbelag in hellen Tönen. Eiche ist das härteste und widerstandsfähigste Holz.

Pour obtenir une sensation de continuité entre la cuisine ouverte et la salle à manger, il faut choisir pour le sol un seul type de revêtement de ton clair. Le chêne est un bois très dur et résistant.

Kies, om een gevoel van doorlopendheid tussen de open keuken en de eetkamer over te dragen, voor een soort plavuizen in een licht tint voor beide ruimtes. Eikenhout is de hardste en duurzaamste houtsoort.

One way to soften the rustic tone of the exposed brick is to paint it white and combine it with natural wood tones.

Eine Art, den rustikalen Eindruck von sichtbaren Ziegelsteinen zu mildern, ist, sie weiß zu streichen und mit Holz in Naturtönen zu verbinden.

Le côté rustique de la brique peut être nuancé en la peignant en blanc et en l'associant à des bois aux tons naturels.

Een manier om het landelijke accent van onbepleisterde baksteen te verminderen, is om het wit te schilderen en te combineren met hout in natuurlijke tinten.

Take advantage of the many possibilities of wood and apply it as wall cladding, either in large expanses or panels that create a decorative texture.

Nutzen Sie die vielen Möglichkeiten von Holz und verwenden Sie es als Wandtäfelung, entweder in großformatigen Platten oder Lamellen, die eine dekorative Oberfläche schaffen.

Le bois se plie à des usages multiples : vous pouvez revêtir les murs avec des grandes planches ou des lambris ayant un effet décoratif assuré.

Benut de talrijke mogelijkheden van hout en gebruik het als muurbekleding, hetzij in grote platen waarmee een decoratieve textuur wordt aangebracht.

Roofs with wooded or metal beams can become an additional decorative element if they are painted to match the rest of the room.

Decken aus Holz- oder Metallbalken können in ein zusätzliches dekoratives Element verwandelt werden, wenn man sie in einer Farbe, die dem übrigen Zimmer entspricht, streicht.

Les plafonds à poutres en bois ou en métal peints avec une couleur qui s'accorde avec le reste de la pièce peuvent devenir un élément de décoration.

Plafonds van houten of metalen balken kunnen een decoratief element worden als ze worden geschilderd in een kleur die past bij de rest van de kamer.

Dark colors can only be used to clad both the walls and ceiling if there is a large window to ensure that light enters.

Ein Zimmer mit derselben Auskleidung an den Wänden und an der Decke erlaubt nur dann dunkle Töne, wenn es große Fenster hat, die Licht einlassen.

Une pièce ayant le même revêtement aux murs et au plafond ne supportera les tons sombres que si elle a de grandes fenêtres assurant l'accès de la lumière.

Een vertrek met dezelfde bekleding op de wanden als het plafond kan donker van kleur zijn als ze grote ramen hebben waardoor de lichtinval gegarandeerd wordt.

To convey a sense of balance, combine floors with
different colors with furniture and fabric in the same
color range.

Um einen Eindruck von Ausgeglichenheit zu vermitteln,
richten Sie die Zimmer, die Böden aus verschiedenfarbigen
Fliesen haben, mit Möbeln und Textilien der gleichen
Farbskala ein.

Pour transmettre une sensation d'équilibre, le carrelage
du sol avec plusieurs couleurs doit s'harmoniser avec des
meubles et des textiles appartenant à la même gamme
de couleur.

Om een gevoel van evenwicht over te dragen kunt u
de kamers uitrusten met tegelvloeren in verschillende
kleuren, meubels en stoffering binnen hetzelfde
kleurengamma.

If the flooring in a room is black the walls and ceilings should be white to enhance the feeling of spaciousness.

In Räumen mit schwarzem Boden, ist es günstig, wenn Wände und Decke weiß sind, um einen weiträumigen Eindruck zu bewirken.

Si la pièce a un sol noir, les parois et le plafond doivent être peints en blanc, pour augmenter la sensation d'espace.

In kamers met een zwarte vloer is het raadzaam om de muren en het plafond wit te houden, om een gevoel van ruimte te geven.

Find the solution that best fits your home. In addition to the traditional claddings, there is an interesting range of materials such as metal and glass bricks.

Suchen Sie die Lösung, die für Ihr Haus am geeignetsten ist. Außer den traditionellen Wandverkleidungen gibt es eine interessante Materialpalette wie Metall oder Glasbausteine.

Si vous recherchez la solution la plus adaptée à votre maison, outre les revêtements traditionnels, il existe une gamme intéressante de matériaux, tels le métal et le béton de verre.

Zoek de oplossing die het meest geschikt is voor uw huis. Naast de traditionele bekledingen bestaat er een interessant gamma van materialen zoals metaal en glasstenen.

Small ceramic tiles, either square or oblong, add richness to the texture of the wall. Vitrified tiles add metallic sheen.

Kleine, quadratische oder längliche Keramikfliesen bereichern die Textur der Wand. Die glasierten Fliesen haben einen metallischen Glanz.

Les petits carreaux en céramique, carrés ou allongés, enrichissent la texture du mur et, vitrifiés, ils ajoutent une brillance métallisée.

Kleine keramiek tegeltjes verrijken, of ze nu vierkant of langwerpig zijn, de textuur van de wand. Met geëmailleerde tegeltjes wordt een metaalachtige glans verkregen.

Make the wall with the mirror stand out by cladding it totally different from the rest of the bathroom.

Heben Sie die Wand, an der sich der Spiegel befindet, durch deine Verkleidung hervor, die sich radikal von dem übrigen Bad unterscheidet.

Vous pouvez faire ressortir le mur où le miroir est accroché avec un revêtement radicalement différent du reste de la salle de bain.

Laat de spiegelwand opvallen met een bekleding die radicaal verschilt van de rest van de badkamer.

All-white bathrooms have little charm. Break the sense of coldness with a pouffe or a black or brown skin rug.

Vollkommen weiße Bäder sind nicht sehr fröhlich. Unterbrechen Sie den Eindruck von Kälte, den sie ausstrahlen, mit einem Puff aus schwarzem oder braunem Leder, oder einem Teppich.

Les salles de bain complètement blanches ont très peu de charme. Vous pouvez casser la sensation de froid qu'elles transmettent avec un pouf ou un tapis en peau noir ou marron.

Helemaal witte badkamers zijn niet erg charmant. Verbreek het koude gevoel die ze uitstralen met een poef of een zwart of bruin leren vloerkleed.

DECO DETAILS
DEKORATIVE DETAILS
DÉTAILS DECO
DECO DETAILS

Do not be afraid to contrast: if you chose a radical color for the wall, be consistent with the choice of ornaments and bold shaped lamps.

Fürchten Sie keine Kontraste: Wenn Sie eine radikale Farbe für die Wand gewählt haben, seinen Sie bei der Auswahl von gewagten Dekorationsgegenständen und Lampen konsequent.

Il ne faut pas avoir peur des contrastes : si vous avez choisi une couleur vive pour le mur, des éléments décoratifs et des lampes aux formes audacieuses confirmeront votre style.

Vrees niet voor contrast: heeft u gekozen voor een radicale kleur op de muur, wees dan consequent in de keuze voor decoraties en lampen in gewaagde vormen.

Do not be afraid to contrast: counteract the cold floor with natural fiber seats or cushions and wool throws.

Fürchten Sie keine Kontraste: Wirken Sie der Fußbodenkälte mit Sitzen oder Kissen aus Naturfasern und Wolldecken entgegen.

Il ne faut pas avoir peur des contrastes : vous pouvez pallier à la froideur du sol avec des sièges ou des coussins en fibre naturelle et des couvertures en laine.

Vrees niet voor contrasten: neutraliseer een koude vloer met zittingen of kussens van natuurvezel en wollen dekens.

If the ornament is very small, combine it with similar pieces of different sizes. This will not take away from its visual impact.

Wenn die Ziergegenstände sehr klein sind, ist es günstig, ähnliche Gegenstände verschiedener Größe zu gruppieren. Wenn nicht, verlieren Sie an Ausdruckskraft.

Si l'élément décoratif est très petit, il vaut mieux créer des ensembles avec des pièces similaires de la même taille, car vous risquez de perdre son impact visuel.

Als een decorstuk heel klein is, is het een idee om een geheel te vormen met gelijksoortige elementen met verschillende afmetingen. Anders vallen ze niet op.

Books can be a decorative element, especially older books. Stack them in order so as they do not seem to have been left there.

Bücher können sehr dekorativ sein, besonders wenn sie alt sind. Sie sollten nur ordentlich aufgestapelt sein, dass sie nicht so aussehen, als ob man sie vergessen hätte.

Les livres, en particulier s'ils sont anciens, peuvent devenir des objets décoratifs. Il faut juste les empiler d'une manière ordonnée pour qu'ils ne donnent pas l'impression d'avoir été oubliés.

Boeken kunnen een decoratief element zijn, vooral als ze oud zijn. Leg ze wel op een nette stapel zodat het niet lijkt alsof ze rondslingeren.

Create a comfy reading corner with a nice bouquet of flowers to help improve mood in a simple and natural way.

Gestalten Sie eine gemütliche Leseecke mit einem hübschen Blumenstrauß, der auf einfache und natürliche Art hilft, die Laune zu heben.

On peut créer un coin lecture accueillant grâce à un bouquet de fleurs, qui aide à détendre l'atmosphère avec simplicité et naturel.

Richt een gezellige leeshoek in met een mooie bos bloemen die op eenvoudige wijze bijdragen aan een goed humeur.

Use colored glass bottles as vases. Just make sure that
they do not have labels or words engraved on the glass,
except in the case of very old bottles that could be
categorized as vintage.

Verwandeln Sie farbige Glasflaschen in Blumenvasen. Sie
dürfen nur keine Etiketten oder ins Glas eingeritzte Worte
haben, es sei denn, dass es sich um sehr alte Flaschen
handelt, die zur *vintage* Kategorie gehören.

Les bouteilles en verre coloré peuvent devenir des vases,
à condition qu'elles n'aient ni étiquette ni inscription
gravée, sauf s'il s'agit de bouteilles très anciennes,
qui rentrent dans la catégorie *vintage*.

Verander gekleurde glazen flessen in vazen. Het enige
vereiste is dat ze geen etiketten of opschriften hebben,
tenzij het gaat om hele oude flessen die in de categorie
vintage vallen.

Decorate the bathroom with natural elements using a very simple minimalist arrangement such as these single leafs.

Dekorieren Sie das Bad mit Elementen aus der Natur mit Hilfe eines minimalistischen, sehr schlichten Arrangement, das nur aus einem großen Blatt besteht.

Vous pouvez décorer votre salle de bain aves des éléments empruntés à la nature, comme cette composition minimaliste très simple constituée d'une seule feuille.

Decoreer de badkamer met elementen uit de natuur op een minimalistische, eenvoudige manier, met uit een blad.

One decorative option is to combine flowers with the wall paint, upholstery or other objects such as pillows, lamps, curtains and carpets.

Eine dekorative Variante ist, die Blumen mit der Farbe der Wand, den Polsterbezügen oder anderen Gegenständen wie Kissen, Lampen, Vorhängen oder Teppichen zu kombinieren.

Vous pouvez varier la décoration en associant les fleurs à la peinture des murs, à la tapisserie ou à d'autres objets comme coussins, lampes, rideaux et tapis.

Een decoratieve variant is om bloemen te combineren met de kleur verf op de muren, de stoffering of voorwerpen zoals kussens, lampen en vloerkleden.

Decorate the windows with prickly pears in small pots
attached using a simple metal bar.

Dekorieren Sie große Fenster mit Kakteen in kleinen
Töpfen, die mit Hilfe einer einfachen Metallleiste befestigt
werden.

Les grandes fenêtres peuvent être décorées avec des
plantes grasses dans des petits pots accrochés à une
simple barre de métal.

Decoreer grote ramen met vijgencactussen in kleine
bloempotten die door middel van een eenvoudige metalen
stang worden opgehangen.

Often the composition of a group of decorative objects is more important than the individual piece. Find a balance between the shapes and colors to create charming corners.

Oft ist die Komposition einer Gruppe von dekorativen Gegenständen wichtiger als die einzelnen Stücke. Suchen Sie das Gleichgewicht von Farben und Formen, um charmante Ecken zu gestalten.

Souvent, la composition d'un groupe d'objets décoratifs est plus marquante que la pièce elle-même. La recherche de l'équilibre des formes et des couleurs est fondamentale pour réussir à créer des coins de charme.

De compositie van een groep decoratieve voorwerpen doet vaak meer dan een afzonderlijk element. Zoek naar evenwicht in vormen en kleuren om gezellige hoekjes in te richten.

Nature is so rich and varied; any element can be used as a decorative object. Use elements such as dried fruit, pine cones and fossils that do not change over time.

Die Natur ist so reich und vielfältig an Formen, man jedes ihrer Elemente in ein Dekorationsobjekt verwandeln kann. Suchen Sie Elemente wie Nüsse, Tannenzapfen und Versteinerungen aus, die sich im Lauf der Zeit nicht verändern.

La nature est si riche et variée en formes que n'importe lequel de ses éléments peut se transformer en objet décoratif. Les fruits secs, les pommes de pin et les fossiles ne s'altèrent pas avec le temps.

De natuur is zo rijk en gevarieerd qua vormen dat willekeurige van haar elementen kunnen veranderen in een decoratief element. Zoek bijvoorbeeld gedroogde vruchten, dennenappels en fossielen die mettertijd niet veranderen.

Cushions are a decorative and practical par excellence.
In addition to style, comfort and provide the ability to
create makeshift seats on the floor.

Kissen sind dekorative und praktische Elemente
schlechthin. Außer zum Stil tragen Sie zur Bequemlichkeit
bei und bieten die Möglichkeit, Sitzgelegenheiten auf dem
Boden zu improvisieren.

Les coussins sont les éléments décoratifs et pratiques par
excellence. Non seulement ils donnent un style, mais ils
apportent aussi du confort et se transforment en sièges
improvisés par terre.

Kussens zijn een decoratief en praktisch element bij
uitstek. Behalve stijl geven ze comfort en de mogelijkheid
om geïmproviseerde zitplaatsen op de grond te creëren.

Play with combinations of shapes and patterns, but always keep a common pattern, which can be a same range of colors or the same type of textures.

Spielen Sie mit der Kombination von Formen und Mustern, aber behalten Sie immer eine gemeinsame Linie bei, die sich in derselben Farbpalette oder in der selben Stoffart ausdrücken kann.

Il est possible de jouer avec les formes et les imprimés, tout en gardant un fil conducteur commun – par exemple, la même gamme de tonalités ou le même type de matière.

Speel met een combinatie van vormen en opdrukken, maar houd altijd een gemeenschappelijke richtsnoer aan. Dit kan hetzelfde kleurengamma of dezelfde soort textuur.

Use cushions in the same range of colors to create well-defined spaces in the garden.

Verwenden Sie Kissen derselben Farbskala, um abgegrenzte Bereiche im Garten zu gestalten.

Utiliser des coussins dans la même gamme de couleurs permet de créer des espaces bien définis dans le jardin.

Gebruik kussens in hetzelfde kleurengamma om goed afgebakende ruimtes in de tuin te creëren.

Place comfortable cushions around a low table to create a dining room area outside the house.

Legen Sie ein paar bequeme Kissen auf den Boden um einen niedrigen Tisch herum, und schaffen Sie so einen Essplatz außerhalb des Hauses.

Des coussins confortables autour d'une table basse créent un coin repas à l'extérieur de la maison.

Leg een aantal comfortabele kussens op de grond rondom een laag tafeltje, om buiten een eethoek in te richten.

Frame illustrations, photos or pictures and hang them on the main walls of the house. If you opt for a composition, check it out on the floor before hanging it on the wall.

Rahmen Sie Poster, Fotos oder Bilder und hängen Sie sie an exponierte Wände des Hauses. Wenn Sie sich für eine Komposition entscheiden, probieren Sie sie vorher auf dem Boden aus.

Vous pouvez encadrer des gravures, des photos ou des dessins et les placer dans les coins clés de la maison. Si vous aimez une composition, il faut l'essayer d'abord au sol.

Lijst prenten, foto's of schilderijen in en zet ze langs de belangrijkste muren van het huis. Heeft u een bepaalde compositie in het hoofd, probeer die dan eerst op de vloer uit.

Small and medium pictures tend to visually get lost in the space. It is better integrate them into a composite supported on a desk, shelf or wall overhang.

Kleine und mittlere Bilder neigen dazu, sich im Raum zu verlieren. Es ist besser sie in einer Gruppe auf einem Möbelstück, in einem Regal oder auf einem Mauervorsprung aufzustellen.

Les tableaux petits et moyens ont tendance à se perdre visuellement dans l'espace. Il vaut mieux les réunir sur un meuble, une étagère ou un décrochement dans le mur.

Kleine en middelgrote schilderijen hebben de neiging om in de ruimte onopgemerkt te blijven. Het is dan beter om ze deel uit te laten maken van een compositie, leunend op een meubelstuk, een plank of een richel tegen de muur.

Enhance the whole concept using the same passe-partout and the same frame.

Verstärken Sie das Ensemble-Konzept, indem Sie gleiche Passepartouts und gleiche Rahmen verwenden.

La notion d'ensemble peut être renforcée en utilisant le même passe-partout et le même cadre.

Versterk het concept van eenheid door gebruik te maken van hetzelfde passepartouts en dezelfde lijst.

Line up several pictures of the same size, frame and
passe-partout to define different environments within
a single room.

Richten Sie mehrere Bilder von gleicher Größe, mit
gleichen Rahmen und gleichem Passepartout in einer Linie
aus, um verschiedene Bereiche im Zimmer zu definieren.

Des tableaux ayant le même format, cadre et passe-
partout peuvent délimiter des espaces consacrés
à des usages différents dans une même pièce.

Hang verschillende schilderijen met dezelfde afmeting,
lijst en passepartouts in een lijn naast elkaar om ruimtes
met een verschillend gebruik binnen dezelfde kamer af
te bakenen.

The bathroom, just like any other room in the house, can be decorated and you can hang pictures provided that the walls are not patterned with prints.

Das Bad kann man, wie jedes andere Zimmer des Hauses, dekorieren und deshalb kann man dort Bilder aufhängen, vorausgesetzt, dass die Wände keine gemusterten Tapeten haben.

On peut décorer la salle de bain comme n'importe quelle autre pièce de la maison : les tableaux sont un excellent choix si les murs n'ont pas de revêtement imprimé.

De badkamer kan, net als ieder ander vertrek in het huis, worden gedecoreerd en daarom kunnen er ook schilderijen worden opgehangen, mits de wanden geen bekleding met opdruk hebben.

Why not hang a picture in the kitchen that is not related to the spaces? Find an image that matches the style of the space.

Schaffen Sie in der Küche mit einem Bild ohne kulinarische Motive einen Überraschungseffekt. Suchen Sie ein Bild, das mit dem Stil dieses Raumes harmoniert.

Un tableau au sujet non culinaire assure un effet de surprise dans la cuisine. L'image doit toutefois s'accorder au style de cette pièce.

Verras in de keuken met een schilderij zonder culinaire motieven. Zoek een afbeelding uit die overeenkomt met de stijl van dit vertrek.

If you have space, take advantage of the worktop to support small pictures but try not to break the harmony of colors in the kitchen.

Wenn Sie Platz haben, nutzen Sie die Spüle, um dort kleine Bilder aufzustellen, aber ohne die Farbharmonie der Küche zu unterbrechen

Si vous avez de la place, vous pouvez poser à côté de l'évier de petits tableaux, respectant l'harmonie des couleurs de la cuisine.

Heeft u ruimte, benut de gootsteen dan als steun voor kleine schilderijen zonder de kleurenharmonie van de keuken te verstoren.

Create a focal point in the room by hanging an image.

Heben Sie die Bedeutung einer Zone eines Zimmers hervor, indem Sie ein Bild dort aufhängen, wohin Sie die Aufmerksamkeit lenken wollen.

Il est possible d'attirer l'attention sur des zones spécifiques de la pièce en les décorant avec une image.

Laat bepaalde delen van een kamer opvallen door er een schilderij op de hangen.

Mirrors are a great resource when you combine pieces of different styles and periods. The contrast between old and new creates a unique atmosphere.

Spiegel bieten ausgezeichnete Möglichkeiten, wenn man Stücke aus verschiedenen Epochen und Stilen kombiniert. Der Kontrast zwischen modern und alt schafft eine einmalige Atmosphäre.

Les miroirs sont un excellent élément si l'on réunit des pièces d'époques et de styles différents. Le contraste entre l'ancien et le moderne crée une atmosphère unique.

Spiegels zijn een uitstekend hulpmiddel als er verschillende exemplaren uit verschillende periodes en met verschillende stijlen worden gecombineerd. Het contrast tussen modern en antiek zorgt voor een unieke sfeer.

Two full-length mirrors flat leaning against the wall create a sophisticated atmosphere in the bedroom.

Zwei auf dem Boden aufgestellte Ganzkörperspiegel schaffen eine raffinierte Umgebung im Schlafzimmer.

Deux miroirs de grande taille posés au sol créent une atmosphère plus sophistiquée dans la chambre à coucher.

Twee passpiegels op de grond geven een verfijnde sfeer in de slaapkamer.

The aesthetic quality of a home depends in part on the individuality of small ornaments that may be antique pieces or from exotic cultures.

Die ästhetische Qualität eines Hauses hängt zum Teil von der Besonderheit kleiner Dekorationsobjekte ab. Das können antike Stücke oder Gegenstände aus exotischen Kulturen sein.

La qualité esthétique d'une maison dépend en partie du caractère exclusif de certains objets – pièces anciennes ou provenant de cultures exotiques.

De esthetische kwaliteit van een woning hangt voor een deel af van de exclusiviteit van kleine decorstukken, zoals antieke voorwerpen of dingen uit exotische culturen.

Use a personal passion to make it into a decorative element. Hats, shoes, souvenirs... any object is valid when it is displayed in an ensemble.

Nutzen Sie eine persönliche Leidenschaft für die Dekoration. Hüte, Schuhe, Reise-*souvenirs* ... Jeder Gegenstand ist geeignet, wenn man ihn in einem Ensemble präsentiert.

Les passions personnelles peuvent devenir des éléments de décoration. Chapeaux, chaussures, souvenirs de voyage... N'importe quel objet peut jouer ce rôle s'il fait partie d'un ensemble.

Maak van een persoonlijke passie een decoratief element. Hoeden, schoenen, *souvenirs* ... alle willekeurig voorwerpen zijn mogelijk als ze als geheel worden gepresenteerd.

Convert the fireplace shelf into a personal still life of objects of different heights without cluttering the shelf.

Arrangieren Sie auf dem Kaminsims mit Objekten verschiedener Höhe ein persönliches Stillleben, ohne es zu überladen.

L'étagère de la cheminée accueille une nature morte personnelle constituée d'objets de tailles variées, sans toutefois que sa surface soit complètement saturée.

Verander de schoorsteenmantel in een steun voor een persoonlijk stilleven met voorwerpen met verschillende hoogtes, zonder de plank te vol te zetten.

Apply a touch of charm with small details that contrast with the predominant textures, like pieces of glass and bright colors to a rustic atmosphere.

Verleihen Sie einer rustikalen Umgebung Charme, mit Details, die mit den vorherrschenden Texturen kontrastieren, wie z.B. leuchtende Farben oder Objekte aus Glas.

Vous pouvez apporter une touche de charme au style rustique grâce à de petits détails qui contrastent avec les matériaux prédominants, tels des objets en verre aux couleurs vives.

Geef ruimtes met een landelijke sfeer nog meer charme met kleine details die contrasteren met overheersende texturen zoals glazen voorwerpen en felle kleuren.

Candles are a great not only for their decorative
appearance but also for the type of light they create.

Kerzen sind sehr dekorativ, nicht nur aufgrund ihres
Aussehens, sondern auch wegen der Art des Lichts,
das sie erzeugen.

Les bougies sont de très bons éléments décoratifs, non
seulement pour leur apparence mais aussi pour le type
d'éclairage qu'elles génèrent.

Kaarsen zijn een goede manier om te decoreren, niet
alleen vanwege hun uiterlijk, maar ook door het soort
verlichting dat ze geven.

Group candles of different heights for greater visual
impact, but they all the same color.

Gruppieren Sie Kerzen von verschiedener Höhe, damit
sie auffallen, sie sollten aber alle die gleiche Farbe haben.

Si vous réunissez des bougies de différentes tailles et
de la même couleur, vous obtiendrez un impact visuel
plus réussi.

Combineer kaarsen van verschillende grootte voor een
betere visuele impact, maar houd wel vast aan een kleur.

Hang glass beads from the ceiling lamp, paint words on the curtain, paste vinyl flowers in a corner of the room or use a collection of small objects to give personality to the rooms.

Hängen Sie Anhänger von Kristallkronleuchtern auf, malen Sie Worte auf die Gardine, kleben Sie Vinylblumen in eine Ecke des Schlafzimmers oder verwenden Sie eine Sammlung kleiner Objekte dafür, diesen Zimmern eine persönliche Atmosphäre zu verleihen.

Pour personnaliser les pièces, vous pouvez accrocher des gouttes de verre au lustre, peindre des mots sur les rideaux, coller des stickers au thème floral dans un coin de la chambre à coucher ou utiliser une collection de petits objets.

Hang glazen kralen aan de plafondlamp, teken woorden op het gordijn, plak vinyl bloemen in een hoekje van de slaapkamer of gebruik een collectie kleine voorwerpen om de vertrekken persoonlijk te maken.

Give cuisine inspired motifs, widely used in kitchen decor, a modern touch by etching them on the glass.

Geben Sie Motiven, die von der Gastronomie inspiriert sind und in der Kücheneinrichtung oft verwendet werden, ein modernes Flair, indem Sie in eine Glasscheibe ätzen.

On donne un air moderne aux motifs s'inspirant de la gastronomie, très utilisés dans la décoration de la cuisine, en les gravant à l'acide sur une surface en verre.

Geef een modern tintje aan motieven die geïnspireerd zijn op de gastronomie en die veelvuldig gebruikt worden in de inrichting van de keuken, door ze af te drukken glas door middel van zuurgraveren.

Cuinar v...

Cuinejar *v intr* Feinejar per la cuina.
Preparant el menjar,
Rentant els plats etc.

Cuiner-a *m f* el qui te per ofici cuina...

Give the most traditional pieces a light-hearted edge.

Injizieren Sie ein bisschen Heiterkeit in die traditionellsten Objekte.

Comment apporter un brin d'insouciance dans les pièces plus traditionnelles.

Geef de meest traditionele elementen iets informeels.

Combine eye-catching tablecloths, with plates with the same design pattern, or are completely white that make the table stand out.

Kombinieren Sie sehr auffallend gemusterte Tischdecken mit Geschirr, das dasselbe Muster trägt, oder mit einem vollkommen weißen Service, das sich vom Tisch optisch abhebt.

Les nappes avec des imprimés très voyants peuvent être accompagnées d'assiettes design ornées des mêmes motifs ou complètement blanches pour qu'elles ressortent sur la table.

Combineer tafelkleden met een heel opvallende opdruk met design borden met hetzelfde motief of helemaal wit, zodat ze op tafel opvallen.

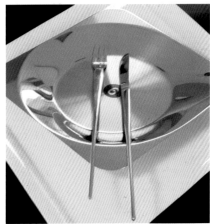

Leave glassware with original shapes and colors in view so that they become decorative elements.

Stellen Sie Designergläser mit originellen Formen und auffallenden Farben als dekorative Objekte sichtbar auf.

Les verres design, aux formes originales et aux couleurs vives, deviennent des objets de décoration.

Laat design glaswerk in het zicht staan, met originele vormen en opvallende kleuren, zodat ze de functie hebben van decoratieve voorwerpen.

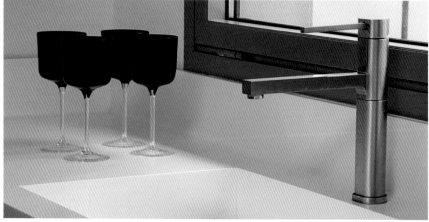

Minimalist ornaments are ideal for the kitchen because they maintain the clean aesthetic required in this space.

Für die Küche sind minimalistische Ziergegenstände geeignet, weil sie die Ästhetik der Sauberkeit, die dieser Raum verlangt, beibehalten.

Les éléments décoratifs minimalistes sont parfaits pour la cuisine, car ils respectent l'esthétique soignée requise par cet espace.

Minimalistische details zijn ideaal voor de keuken omdat ze de esthetiek en netheid die in deze ruimte vereist zijn intact laten.

In industrial-style kitchens or kitchens with one predominant color, apply touches of color using gadgets and exposed dishes.

In Küchen von industriellem Zuschnitt oder in denen, in denen ein einziger Farbton vorherrscht, bringen Sie eine farbige Note durch *gadgets* und Schüsseln, die Sie sichtbar aufstellen.

Dans les cuisines en style industriel ou dominées par une seule couleur, les gadgets et la vaisselle, laissés à l'extérieur, apportent des touches de couleur.

Breng in de keukens met een industrieel ontwerp of waar een enkele toon overheerst kleurrijke accenten aan door *gadgets* en schalen in het zicht te zetten.

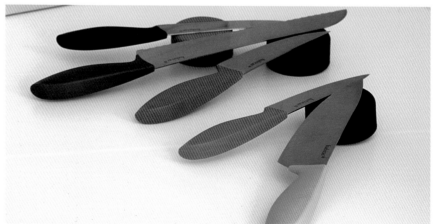

Don't go for elaborate decorations. A sprig of rosemary or very tiny flowers around the napkin are enough to add a delicate touch at the table.

Vermeiden Sie sehr aufwendige Verzierungen. Ein kleiner Rosmarin- oder Blütenzweig neben der Serviette reicht aus, um dem Tisch einen eleganten Hauch zu verleihen.

Il faut éviter les décorations très élaborées. Un brin de romarin ou des petites fleurs posées à côté de la serviette suffiront à apporter une note délicate à votre table.

Vermijd gekunstelde decoratieve voorwerpen. Een takje rozemarijn of kleine bloemen bij het servet is voldoende om op de tafel een subtiel accent aan te brengen.

Not all elements on a table have to be combined exactly. The mixture of styles creates more attractive ensembles. It is only important to avoid sharp contrasts of color.

Nicht alle Elemente eines Tisches müssen ganz genau zueinander passen. Eine Stilmischung schafft attraktivere Zusammenstellungen. Es ist nur wichtig, starke Farbkontraste zu vermeiden.

Tous les éléments d'une table ne doivent pas aller parfaitement ensemble. Le mélange de styles crée des effets plus intéressants. Il faut juste éviter les contrastes de couleurs excessifs.

Niet alle elementen van een tafel hoeven exact te combineren. Een mengeling van stijlen geeft juist een aantrekkelijk geheel. Vermijd alleen grote kleurcontrasten.

To give a few rooms of the house a Provencal air, display white porcelain dishes and wicker baskets, which are very practical.

Um einigen Räumen im Haus einen Hauch der Provence zu verleihen, stellen Sie weiße Schüsseln und Strohkörbchen auf, sie sind außerdem sehr praktisch.

La vaisselle en porcelaine blanche et les paniers en osier, très pratiques, donnent un air provençal à certains endroits de la maison.

Zet praktische, witte porseleinen schalen en rieten manden neer voor een Provençaals accent in bepaalde vertrekken van de woning.

Place pots in wooden crates, crocheted covers or instead use a brass watering can.

Stellen Sie Blumentöpfe in Holzkästen oder gehäkelte Hüllen oder ersetzen Sie sie durch eine Messinggießkanne.

Vous pouvez utiliser comme cache-pot des caisses en bois, des housses faites au crochet ou bien un arrosoir en laiton.

Plaats bloempotten in houten kisten, gehaakte hoezen of vervang ze door een messing gieter.

Make doors stand out with unusual handles, whether old-style wrought iron or a piece of hanging glass.

Heben Sie die Türen durch besonders gestaltete Klinken, entweder aus Schmiedeeisen nach altem Stil oder mit einem hängenden Glastropfen, hervor.

Les portes peuvent être valorisées par des poignées particulières, à l'ancienne en fer forgé ou ornées d'un pendentif en verre.

Laat deuren opvallen door middel van een deurknop met een bijzonder ontwerp, bijvoorbeeld van smeedwerk in oude stijl of met een glazen onderdeel eraan.

Decorate the bathroom with necklaces, bracelets and earrings hanging from a small floor stand or from the edge of the mirror.

Dekorieren Sie das Bad mit Halsketten, Armbändern und Ohrringen, die an einem kleinen Ständer oder am Spiegelrahmen hängen.

Vous pouvez décorer la salle de bain avec des colliers, des bracelets et des pendentifs accrochés à un support sur pied ou au cadre du miroir.

Richt de badkamer in door kettingen, armbanden en oorbellen aan een kleine staander of aan de rand van de spiegel te hangen.

Shells are ideal for decorating the bathroom, not only for
their obvious resistance to moisture but also for creating
a marine environment.

Schneckenhäuser und Muscheln sind ideal, um das Bad
zu dekorieren, nicht nur wegen ihrer offensichtlichen
Resistenz gegen Feuchtigkeit, sondern auch weil sie
Assoziationen an das Meer hervorrufen.

Les coquillages s'adaptent bien à la décoration de la salle
de bain : ils résistent à l'humidité et ils évoquent le milieu
marin.

Slakkenhuizen en schelpen zijn ideaal om de badkamer
mee te versieren, niet alleen vanwege hun evidente
vochtbestendigheid, maar ook vanwege de associatie
met de zee die zij oproepen.

As in spas or hotels, rolls hand towels and leave them in view the creating different combinations of colors.

Wie in den *spas* oder Hotels rollen Sie die Handtücher zusammen und legen Sie sie nach Farben geordnet sichtbar aus.

Comme dans les spas ou dans les hôtels, vous pouvez rouler les serviettes et les laisser à l'extérieur, formant ainsi des compositions de couleurs.

Rol gastenhanddoekjes op, net als in *spa's* of hotels, en leg ze in het zicht, zo dat ze kleurencomposities vormen.